RETIREMENT
RESCUE

RONALD A. GELOK
AND THOMAS J. SMITH

RETIREMENT
RESCUE

*A Consumer's Guide to Protecting Yourself
and Your Family from Out Of Control Taxes and
Roller Coaster Financial Markets*

Published by Advantage, Charleston, South Carolina.
Member of Advantage Media Group.

ADVANTAGE is a registered trademark and the Advantage colophon is a trademark of Advantage Media Group, Inc.

Printed in the United States of America.

ISBN: 978-159932-324-4
LCCN: 2013936403

This publication is designed to provide accurate and authoritative information in regard to the subject matter covered. It is sold with the understanding that the publisher is not engaged in rendering legal, accounting, or other professional services. If legal advice or other expert assistance is required, the services of a competent professional person should be sought.

 Advantage Media Group is proud to be a part of the Tree Neutral® program. Tree Neutral offsets the number of trees consumed in the production and printing of this book by taking proactive steps such as planting trees in direct proportion to the number of trees used to print books. To learn more about Tree Neutral, please visit www.treeneutral.com. To learn more about Advantage's commitment to being a responsible steward of the environment, please visit www.advantagefamily.com/green

Advantage Media Group is a leading publisher of business, motivation, and self-help authors. Do you have a manuscript or book idea that you would like to have considered for publication? Please visit www.amgbook.com or call 1.866.775.1696

TABLE OF CONTENTS

INTRODUCTION

Who Needs Retirement, Estate, and Tax Planning?

I n today's society, there are basically two groups of people entering retirement: the pensionless and those fortunate enough to have pensions. It seems that people who are retiring from government jobs or education-related jobs are most often in the pensioner group. It is not unusual to come across a husband and wife who are both retiring schoolteachers, for example, each of them with a pension and Social Security. Between their two pensions and Social Security, the couple's retirement income needs are often largely met.

I know of one couple in that position: Jerry and Janice, who are retiring in their mid-sixties after careers as high-school teachers. As they are building up those pensions, employees like high-school teachers frequently accumulate hundreds of thousands of dollars in 403(b) plans or tax-sheltered annuity plans through working for the school system. Often, the money saved through those plans ends up not being required to meet current income needs, so people like Jerry and Janice end up taking nothing out of their 403(b) plans, which can be rolled over to IRAs, until they turn seventy-and-one-half years old. The government compels account holders of 403(b) plans and IRAs to begin making their minimum required-distribution withdrawals after turning seventy-and-one-half.

At that point in time, the following question comes up: "What do I do with this required distribution if I do not need it to pay the cable TV bill or the electric bill, or to put groceries on the table?" Many people who have pensions recognize that their adult children may be working at occupations that are ultimately not going to leave them with a pension. Thus, many of these retired parents want to know the answers to the following questions: "How can we benefit our children and grandchildren if we have an asset in the form of a retirement account? How do we maximize the value of that asset for our family?"

Jerry and Janice had this very problem. As they explained to me, "We have this 403(b) account, but we've been reluctant to take money out of it because anything we take out of it is subject to income tax. Now the government is forcing us to take money out. We're not too excited about taking the required minimum distribution and putting that in a low-yield savings account or in some sort of risk-based investment that might make or lose money. What could we do to optimize this asset's value?"

I made a suggestion: "Say we take $10,000 a year, and we gift that into a type of specialized trust set up by an estate-planning attorney. That would potentially enable you to pass hundreds of thousands of dollars, estate- and income-tax-free, to your children. Would that be of interest to you?" Their answer was yes; that was exactly the kind of thing they wanted to do.

Using that strategy, this husband and wife, while in their seventies, were able to create more than $500,000 of tax-free death benefits by using a second-to-die life insurance policy that would pay out in excess of $500,000 when the second policyholder passed away. When this type of trust owns the policy and the trustee follows certain basic rules, the money can be both estate- and income-tax-free to the trust beneficiaries, who are typically the adult children and/or grandchildren of the people who set up and put gifts into the trust.

It gets more interesting than that, though. For this couple, suppose they roll their 403(b) account into an IRA. This method is usually desirable because it opens up many choices for positioning the IRA, compared to leaving it in an employer-sponsored plan, in which the choices are typically much more limited. In addition, every dime of money that comes out of that retirement account is subject to income tax at seemingly ever-increasing tax rates. As a result, some might prefer to transform that "tax-infested" retirement account into an income-tax-free account, such as a Roth IRA.

One way in which people might do that is through a Roth conversion. However, to the extent that such people have significant income coming from pensions and Social Security, converting a six-figure IRA into a Roth is likely to propel them into a higher tax bracket. According to the tax law that went into effect on January 1, 2013, that federal income tax rate can be as high as 39.6 percent. Many states also impose state income tax, which can be anywhere from 2 to 11 percent or more, on top of the federal income tax. So, for a retiree who receives more than adequate income from a pension and Social Security, undertaking a Roth conversion may not be particularly attractive because of the potentially enormous tax cost a conversion would instigate.

However, if financial planners work with retirees to help create hundreds of thousands of tax-free dollars that are potentially estate- and income-tax-free, those retirees' children may have the option to do what's called a *post-death* or *postmortem Roth conversion.* Jerry and Janice had told me, "Our income needs are essentially met because of our pensions and Social Security. We're concerned about our children and grandchildren having as good a quality of life and retirement as we've enjoyed." For people like them, repositioning money in this way can be very advantageous.

Now, let's talk about Harry, another client who is typical of many retirees today. In my opinion, Harry's situation represents that of the vast majority of retirees because of the move toward a pensionless society. As few as thirty years ago, about 82 percent of people who were retiring could count on pension paychecks for life: mailbox money every month. Harry's parents' generation had it very easy when it came to retirement-income planning. They had their pension checks coming in every month, and it seemed that all they had to do was shop around for the highest CD rates.

Harry, in contrast, does not have a pension. Like many people who moved around from job to job in corporate America, he has a few 401(k) accounts that he accumulated while working for several different employers. He recognizes that he cannot live a comfortable retirement lifestyle on Social Security alone. His biggest concern, as he expresses it, is, "How do I make sure I do not run out of income before I run out of breath?" That is a legitimate worry, because people's average lifespans are increasing. Harry, who is sixty years old, could very well live twenty-five years or longer in retirement. If, as is very common, his wife is a few years younger than he is, she may have thirty years or more to live in retirement. The challenge then is how to try and help ensure that the family's accumulated retirement savings last as long as Harry and his wife do.

Recently, I read an article in an investment journal that suggested the standard 4 percent withdrawal rate on retirement savings is being rethought. That number refers to what has been the conventional retirement-planning model for the last twenty-five years. This conventional model rested on the assumption that if a couple has a balanced retirement portfolio, they can comfortably withdraw funds at a rate of 4 percent and not worry about running out of money before dying. This article's author suggested that 4 percent might be too high a withdrawal rate; perhaps a more realistic rate for a couple with a balanced portfolio should be 3.5 percent or less, according to a combination of factors. The first factor, of course, is the increased longevity discussed above. The second factor is increased volatility in the equity or stock markets, and the third factor is record-low yields in the bond markets.

Harry's concern, if he's a do-it-yourself retirement planner who is following conventional wisdom on retirement withdrawals – "Just design this balanced portfolio and everything should turn out okay" – is that the stock and bond markets will not cooperate. They certainly have not been very cooperative recently, and that market volatility, combined with basement-level interest rates, is enough to give Harry some sleepless nights.

The key here for Harry's retirement security is to identify the *income gap*. In other words, if Harry has a certain amount of regular, predictable monthly expenditures while he is in retirement and his income is based upon his Social Security, then a financial planner first needs to identify the gap between what is needed to cover Harry and his wife's expenses, which will allow them to live the lifestyle they want to live, and their Social Security income. Can the financial planner position enough retirement savings to fill that income gap?

This is the type of case in which a financial planner can use different vehicles to create income, including vehicles that do not have a direct correlation to the stock or bond markets. For example, today people can take advantage of fixed annuities that offer lifetime income guarantees without requiring annuitization. In the past, if someone wanted a guaranteed income for life, he or she might trade a lump sum of money to an insurance company for an immediate annuity, or stream of payments, that would last for the rest of his or her life. The drawback to that approach is that the individual receiving the annuity loses control of the lump sum because, in effect, he or she has traded the lump sum away in exchange for the stream of payments from the insurance company. What if the individual should need that lump sum? In the past, he or she would have been out of luck.

Today, the insurance industry offers innovative, useful products in the area of annuities that makes those annuities much more attractive and exciting to folks looking to create their own perpetual, pension-like income stream that is guaranteed for life. An individual can still purchase an annuity that can guarantee him or her a lifetime income, but, in addition, he or she will have access to a lump sum in the event of an emergency. Furthermore, if the account holder passes away, a lump sum typically passes to named beneficiaries. That is completely liquid money. For somebody like Harry, this annuity offering fulfills the need for that pension-like, regular income stream without the unpleasant limitations of former annuity programs.

Finally, let's talk about Bob and Terri, who are also typical of a segment of today's retiree population. These are people who have succeeded beyond their own expectations. When people have created millions of dollars in assets, often they want those assets to benefit their loved ones – and why not? Most people, whether they are middle-class, upper-middle-class, or wealthy, feel that if they have worked for a lifetime to accumulate assets, then those assets should benefit their children and grandchildren; the government should not take those assets away from their family and redistribute their money to other people's children and grandchildren. They have worked hard for their money, and they do not want to gift it to Uncle Sam. In other words, this is the issue of the estate tax, and the federal estate tax in particular, though many states have estate taxes as well. As of January 1, 2013, the federal estate-tax exemption threshold is $5,250,000, and it is indexed for inflation. Any estate valued at more than $5,250,000 will be taxed at a 40-percent rate when money passes to the next generation. Depending upon the state of residency, heirs may experience a significant state estate-tax bite. For example, in New Jersey, estates of more than $675,000 are subject to state estate taxes in addition to federal estate taxes. In addition, do not forget the fact that every penny in tax-qualified accounts, such as IRAs and 401(k) accounts, is also subject to income tax when it is removed from those accounts. To complicate matters, the federal estate-tax threshold is what some would call a moving target. It has changed 12 times in the last fifteen years and came very close to being adjusted to just $1,000,000 on January 1, 2013. Can anyone predict with accuracy where the threshold may be set by a subsequent group of politicians ten to twenty years in the future?

In Bob and Terri's situation, their issue is how they can minimize the impact of estate taxes on their family and how they can maximize the amount of money that they can pass along to benefit their family.

Currently, a unique opportunity exists for wealth transfer planning: people can gift up to $5,000,000 without incurring a gift tax. So, right now, Bob and Terry might decide, "If we're worth $10,000,000, we can take $5,000,000 and gift that into a specialized type of family trust."

Where the trustee puts that money then becomes the challenge. If the trustee puts that money in CDs, the money is going to grow at a snail's pace. If the trustee puts the money into bonds, and interest rates go up, the value of the bonds is likely to go backward. If the trustee puts the money into stocks or equities, the money might go up in value, but it might go down in value, too.

Once again, if a financial planner helps them with *wealth-transfer planning*, Bob and Terry could gift $5,000,000 to their trust and have their accountant file a gift tax return. If they are in their early to mid-sixties, that $5,000,000 could be turned into a $30,000,000 or more life insurance policy or death benefit, depending on their health status, with a one-time payment. With this type of planning, they would be able to keep a lid on the growth of their taxable estate by moving a significant portion of their money outside the taxable estate through the gift to the trust. Their accountant would have to file a gift tax return, but no tax liability would be due on that gift. This is a technique that can be used to enable financially successful people to maximize the amount of money that will benefit family members, as opposed to being redistributed by the government via federal and state estate tax.

As you might guess, I deal with a broad range of clients who have very different needs and income levels. I work with them all to help them make smart choices for their particular situations. I think what separates a good adviser from many other advisers is that a good adviser will listen to what people say is most important to them about their money, their life, or their family. Then, a skilled adviser will work with those people to design a plan that is consistent with what they value and what is important to them. Frequently, I see advisers fall back on textbook answers to suggest plans to clients, but textbook answers do not always offer the best real-world solutions.

What I bring to the table is many years of experience in doing planning for older people and their families. In particular, I bring valuable insights to the tax aspects of retirement planning because my background is that of a tax and estate attorney. I have drafted wills; I have drafted trusts; and I have done planning from the legal perspective. Now, I offer another focus from the financial-planning perspective. I am able to talk intelligently with a client's team of advisers and family members, and I come up with planning that often makes sense to the client's adviser, accountant, and banker, as well as the client him- or herself.

Unfortunately, in today's society, that knowledge has gotten extremely specialized. Sometimes a person may talk to his accountant, but the accountant does not communicate with the financial adviser, who, in turn, does not communicate with the tax attorney or the estate-planning attorney. I have the expertise to communicate with my clients and their other advisers; moreover, if my clients do not have those other advisers, I am able to introduce them to advisers with whom they may want to work with regard to accounting, banking, or specialized areas of advanced planning.

I came to this expertise via years of university education and real-world experience. I have observed people who try to be everything to everybody but are unable to do so. For example, if a person spends his or her entire career working in a banking environment, then he or she is just going to have a banker's perspective. If an individual spends his or her career exclusively in an accounting firm, then he or she will be largely the product of that environment and have an accountant's perspective. Alternatively, if an individual spends his or her entire career drafting wills and trusts, then he or she will have an estate-planning attorney's perspective. Don't get me wrong; all of these perspectives are valuable, but each of them has limitations. Because my education and prior work experience are so varied, I am able to bring multiple perspectives and considerations to the table, and clients seem to find this extremely valuable. Clients have told me that it is a pleasure to work with me. They have shared their frustrations at having met with other advisers who could answer no questions outside their area(s) of basic competency.

Clients today deserve and demand more. For example, clients often have questions about the planning considerations required when they own property in more than one jurisdiction or state. Suppose a person owns a primary residence in New Jersey and a second residence in Florida. Suppose, too, that this individual owns a timeshare in Nevada and another timeshare in California. Many people do not understand that real estate, including deeded time-share interests, goes through probate in the state in which it is located. In the example I just gave, that means four different probates in four different states. These multiple probates could be avoided by doing proper planning. Sometimes we do not know what we do not know. That is why seeking out the right advisers is so important. (If we ever start to work together, be sure to ask me for a copy of *The Consumer's Guide to Finding the Right Advice-Givers.* That can save you many headaches down the road.)

When choosing advisers with whom to work, try to find individuals who are passionate about what they do. One of the worst things is when an individual finds himself or herself working with someone who views what he or she does as a job, rather than a career. People who own their own businesses often care more about their clients than the employees of a large firm do. In addition, ask your potential adviser how many hours he or she spends each year in continuing education. Consider whether the adviser with whom you might work is so dedicated that he or she is a published author in his or her field. Then, there is the issue of passion. I think that when people work at what they are passionate about, they are far more likely to be successful than if they work at something they do not enjoy.

What I am passionate about is helping people with their retirement-income planning, helping people with ideas to minimize their taxes, helping people so that they do not have to worry so much about their financial security in retirement, and helping them to pass as much money as possible in the most tax-advantageous way to their family down the road. Right now, many people are extremely frustrated by trying to figure out how to position retirement savings or IRAs intelligently. People have said to me, "Gee, I just don't know what to do or what direction to turn. I know if I put too much of my retirement account funds in individual stocks or stock-based mutual funds and we have another big downturn, I could lose 30 or 35 percent of that portion of my IRA. At this stage of the game, now that I'm retired, I don't want to take that kind of risk. At the same time, I know that if I put too much of my IRA into bonds right now, with interest rates being at a fifty-year low, then I stand to lose principal if I cash in my bonds when interest rates go back up. And I'm not excited about the pathetically low interest rates available in banks' CDs."

These days, we sometimes refer to CDs as "certificates of disappointment" or "certificates of disillusionment" because of the ultralow interest rates that CDs are paying. It is all frustrating to retirees, who see that too much in stocks exposes them to potentially devastating down-side risk, too much in bonds can do the same, and rates on CDs are nowhere near what it takes to keep up with inflation. If too much reliance on bonds is not the answer, too much reliance on stocks is not the answer, and too much reliance on bank CDs is not the answer, what else can people look to for that portion of retirement savings when they want to limit or reduce risk? I cover that and much more in the chapters to come.

CHAPTER ONE

Taxing Times

W hat is happening with income-tax rates? Who will be impacted? What changes can we expect to see in income tax, dividend taxes, estate taxes, and capital gains taxes?

On January 1, 2013, Congress acted to change the tax law in many ways. Many people are wondering what these changes are and how those changes potentially impact them going forward. They want to know how the changes affect them. For a start, Congress has enacted an increase in income-tax rates on the upper end of the spectrum. This impacts individuals earning over $400,000 and married couples earning over $450,000. In 2012, those high earners fell under a maximum federal income-tax bracket of 35 percent. In 2013 and following, the new maximum bracket is 39.6 percent. Another change is that individuals who have 401(k) accounts can do Roth conversions of those 401(k) accounts, which they were previously not allowed to do.

As for capital gains, long-term capital gains, and dividends, Congress has scheduled changes to occur there as well. For those high-income wage earners who are in the 39.6-percent income-tax bracket, long-term capital gains, which are currently taxed at a rate of 15 percent, will be taxed at a rate of 20 percent as of January 1, 2013. For earners who fall under the 39.6-percent income-tax bracket, dividends, which are currently taxed at the same rate as long-term capital gains, will be taxed at 15 percent; for earners in the 39.6-percent income-tax rate or higher, dividends will be taxed at a rate of 20 percent. These are significant increases, especially for high-income wage earners, retirees, and pre-retirees. Suppose you are a retiree in the new 39.6-percent income-tax bracket. Suppose you derive a meaningful portion of your retirement income from dividends and that those dividends are currently taxed at 15 percent. When the 35-percent rate moves to 39.6 percent, it means that your income-tax rate moves up, too. Those dividends, which formerly were taxed at 15 percent, now get taxed at 20 percent, which is a much higher rate of taxation. In addition, do not forget about the new 3.8-percent tax on investments for individuals earning over $200,000 and for married couples making over $250,000. Congress designed this new tax to help fund a new healthcare law: the Affordable Care Act.

Congress has also made changes to federal estate taxes; the federal estate-tax exclusion for 2012 was $5,120,000 and changed to $5,250,000 on January 1, 2013. This change means that any estate worth more than $5,250,000 will be taxed at a new 40-percent rate when that estate passes to the next generation. The estate tax does not apply between spouses. There is some speculation that Congress may act to change this again in the future, but it is difficult to know if and when the estate-tax exclusion will change again (aside from the fact that it is now indexed for inflation). Right now, in my opinion, it is difficult to imagine Republicans and Democrats agreeing on anything.

What is even more difficult to predict is exactly where the federal estate-tax will be in relation to life expectancy. If somebody is seventy-two years old and has a life expectancy of another fifteen years, that person cannot gauge for sure where the federal estate-tax threshold will be in fifteen years. That is because the estate-tax threshold has been a moving target, with Congress continually tinkering with it. The best thing anyone can do is to plan ahead of time to address this issue based on an understanding of the current law.

CHAPTER TWO

Dodging the Bullets

N ow that you know large amounts of your hard-earned money may be squarely in the government's sights, what can you do to protect that money?

Some solutions fall into the category of legal document solutions, while others would be more accurately described as financial-planning solutions. Now, the purpose of this book is not to give specific legal advice to anybody. It would be appropriate to discuss what I am about to lay out here with your tax and/or estate attorney, accountant, or another professional adviser.

The number-one tool available to married couples is what termed an *estate-planned will,* which, essentially, is a will that includes trust provisions that create a trust upon the death of the first spouse for the benefit of the surviving spouse. The surviving spouse can be the trustee of this trust. According to the eyes of the law, there are "natural" people and "non-natural" people. For example, a living, breathing person is a "natural" person. A corporation, an LLC, or a trust is an example of a "non-natural" person. As far as the internal revenue code goes, a "non-natural" person is still a person. When the first spouse passes away, the will creates a *testamentary trust,* which means a trust that goes into effect upon the death of the *testator,* or the person who drafted the will. This trust is often referred to as a *marital trust;* assets that go into the marital trust do so for the benefit of the surviving spouse. When assets go into the marital trust, the trust gets its own estate-tax exemption, which can effectively double the amount that the two spouses can leave their children, free of estate tax. For example, in New Jersey the state estate tax impacts estates of more than $675,000. In New York, the state estate tax impacts estates over $1 million. By creating a marital trust, in effect, in New Jersey, a couple can ensure that $1,350,000 of their estate is not subject to state estate tax. In New York, this would be $2 million not subject to estate tax. Moreover, on the federal level, as of 2013, using a properly implemented marital trust means that instead of $5,250,000 not being subject to federal estate tax, about $10.5 million is not subject to federal estate tax.

Please do not put off implementing this type of plan. A couple of years ago, I explained to two of my clients, a married couple, how a marital trust could benefit them and their family. I walked them over to talk with an estate-planning attorney. My clients decided that a marital trust was a great idea; however, since summer was about to start and they were planning to spend most of their summer at the beach, they would wait and establish the trust when they returned to town after Labor Day. Unfortunately, later that summer the husband suffered a fatal stroke. The couple's opportunity to double their amount of money not subject to estate taxes was lost forever. Clearly, the lesson here is that for this type of estate planning, procrastination is unwise.

This type of trust planning can be done through a will or as part of a *revocable living trust.* In some states, probate is burdensome, time-consuming, and costly; in such cases, a client may want to accomplish the same doubling effect by creating a marital trust that is part of a revocable living trust. This is an area in which people generally should not want to do things themselves. Instead, an individual will want to work with a qualified tax- and estate-planning attorney. Ideally, this attorney should be someone who communicates with that individual's financial adviser and tax preparer to establish a coordinated, integrated approach to the estate.

Beyond this type of planning, more sophisticated planning can and often should be done to deal with the issue of federal and state estate taxes. A different type of trust, known as an *irrevocable trust,* can be set up. Now, an irrevocable trust, as its name implies, is a trust that cannot be revoked once set up. While the holder of the trust can stop funding it if he or she so chooses, he or she cannot change the terms of the trust once it is in place. Often, an individual will set up an irrevocable trust for purposes of gifting assets into that trust.

Once people realize they are not likely to spend all of their assets while living, it becomes appropriate for them to consider the use of the irrevocable trust. This is because an individual can, in effect, build a nontaxable estate or asset through the irrevocable trust . With a properly structured trust and adherence to legal requirements, there will be no federal or state estate tax due on that trust when assets pass out of that trust to the trust beneficiaries,

One popular technique is to gift money each year to the trust. The trustee of the trust (often a trusted family member, such as an adult son or daughter), writes a check once a year to a life insurance company for second-to-die life insurance. Let me return to this idea, first mentioned in the introduction, in more detail here.

Take the example of a husband and wife, each seventy years old, who enjoy average health for their age. If they devote $10,000 a year to this play, they may buy themselves more than $500,000 worth of death benefits in a second-to-die survivorship life insurance policy. If they live for twenty years after embarking upon this plan, they will have gifted $200,000 to their trust, which is going to pay out an amount in excess of $500,000. That $500,000, when paid out, would be completely free of estate and income taxes, which could be of tremendous benefit to the couple's family.

Even when the estate size is not large enough to create an enormous projected estate-tax liability, the funds in an irrevocable trust could still be used for another worthy purpose, such as the post-death Roth conversion. Income-tax rates are going up; in my opinion, considering the government's fiscal problems, that trend is likely to continue. It does not take a rocket scientist to realize that the money growing or building in IRAs and 401(k) accounts is likely to be subject to ever-increasing income-tax rates when it is withdrawn. In February 2012, Senator Max Baucus, head of the Senate Finance Committee, introduced a bill that would compel accelerated taxation of inherited IRAs by non-spousal beneficiaries. While it did not pass on that occasion, Baucus's proposal could certainly be reintroduced in Congress's next session.

Suppose you would really like your tax-infested, traditional IRA to be transformed into a tax-free account. In that case, you could do a Roth conversion of that account and move it from a traditional IRA to a tax-free Roth IRA. This process has some requirements and restrictions: a Roth IRA must exist for five years before its account holder can withdraw tax-free funds. Another potential complication for many people, especially people with large IRAs or 401(k) accounts, is the *conversion tax,* which is an income tax on the amount that is being converted. Thus, for example, if a $500,000 IRA is converted in 2013, that IRA may be subject to federal income taxes at a 39.6-percent rate. If the IRA is converted in the future, it may be subject to even higher federal taxes. In addition, depending on an individual's state of residence, he or she may incur state income taxes on that IRA. As a result, for a typical individual, a large Roth conversion during his or her lifetime is not an attractive proposition. In contrast, if the holder of an IRA is compelled to take required minimum distributions from that IRA (distributions that are not needed to pay the bills or to buy groceries), then he or she can certainly use some of those distributions to fund gifting to his or her irrevocable trust.

Suppose a couple have an irrevocable trust that provides a payout of $500,000, or more, that is completely income-tax-free and estate-tax-free upon the death of the surviving spouse. To the extent that the funds are not needed to handle estate-tax liability, they become available for a post-death or postmortem Roth conversion, which could be extremely valuable in the long-term for the children, grand-children, or other ultimate beneficiaries of the IRA.

When a properly set up, traditional IRA is inherited, the heir or heirs have no lump-sum income tax due. This is because the IRA can be "stretched" under current law. What that means is that an inherited IRA can be structured so that the beneficiaries simply take out the required minimum distributions while they are alive. When a properly set up Roth IRA is inherited, the beneficiaries will have to take required minimum distributions, but those required minimum distributions are tax-free. In other words, these approaches incorporate tax-advantaged, multigenerational distribution planning for retirement accounts.

The idea here is to start doing tax planning for retirement accounts or retirement assets in addition to doing tax planning for oneself. How a plan should be crafted all depends on the individual's overall picture: his or her level of income and level of assets will dictate what choices will be most effective. For example, some people want to stop paying income taxes on interest earnings that they are not currently spending. So, for those individuals, the solution might be as simple as developing a tax-deferred annuity. With a tax-deferred annuity, there are no 1099 forms arriving on any of the interest earnings as they accumulate; moreover, the interest earnings are only subject to taxes when the annuity owner chooses to withdraw those earnings at some future point. For other folks, such as those who have estate tax and other issues to consider, planning takes a different direction.

Estate planning may seem like a great deal of trouble; it may seem expensive or confusing. However, the bottom line is that the government has a plan for people who do not do the best possible estate planning; this plan, essentially, is to take more of your assets through taxation than perhaps those people would wish. When the government takes people's money, it does, in part, spend those dollars through tax-funded social welfare programs. This means the money is spent on other people's children, rather than the original people's children and grandchildren. You can choose not to be a victim of what some would consider confiscatory or predatory taxation. You can choose to do proper planning.

Regarding the topic of life insurance, most people have, over the years, read articles in various financial magazines full of advice about getting the least expensive term insurance available during the peak responsibility years, when the children are young and the mortgage balance is large. When the mortgage is paid off and the children's education funded, the writers of these articles advise getting rid of the life insurance because it is an unnecessary expense at that point. For people who are accustomed to thinking that way, the idea of buying some sort of permanent insurance to save on taxes down the road may seem somewhat counterintuitive. I had one client whose parents lived into their early nineties. My client and I became concerned about future estate taxes on my client's estate if she lived as long or nearly as long as her parents had. She was divorced, so we could not use second-to-die life insurance. Instead, we used single life insurance, and we designed a policy that had a death benefit of about $700,000. Half a year later, she suffered a fatal heart attack in a restaurant. Even though the funds were not used to handle a future estate-tax liability, nonetheless, she had made one premium payment, which meant the insurance company paid out $700,000 to the trust. The trust went to benefit her adult children, who were the trust beneficiaries. Their proceeds were free of estate and income taxes.

The other area in which life insurance can be useful is in dealing with catastrophic illness. Illness has become a bit of a problem area for financial planners. In the past, financial planners would simply recommend traditional, long-term-care insurance to clients. What we found was that only 5 percent of retirees implement traditional long-term-care insurance; in many cases, the premiums for a couple can run into thousands of dollars per year. As a result, 95 percent of people pass on or skip long-term-care insurance. It is not that people do not like what long-term-care insurance can do for them, such as helping to pay the cost of home healthcare, assisted living, or even nursing-home care. It is that they do not like or cannot afford paying for the annual premiums.

Traditional long-term-care insurance has become problematic because the premium rates are not guaranteed. Now, back during the time when they sold many long-term-care insurance policies, agents would tell prospective clients, truthfully, that the company had never had a premium increase, but that they reserved the right to raise rates in the future if they raised rates for everybody.

However, policyholders' utilization of long-term-care services has turned out to be far in excess of what many actuaries had predicted. As a result, company after company has gone to state regulators to ask for premium increases on long-term care. Recently, a client showed me a letter he had received from the long-term-care insurance company with which he had had a policy for the previous five years. The letter notified him that his premium would soon increase by 52 percent. This uncertainty about rates is why many retirees are finding traditional long-term-care insurance increasingly unattractive. One problematic scenario occurs when the death of the primary pensioner causes a loss of income. For example, suppose a husband and wife hold a long-term-care policy, and the husband passes away. The surviving spouse loses the smaller of the couple's two Social Security payments, and often his or her pension income is reduced too. So, when one of the surviving spouse's Social Security payments stops and his or her pension income is cut by, say, one-third or one-half, if that surviving spouse gets a double-digit premium increase on his or her traditional long-term-care insurance, that insurance may become unaffordable, and he or she may have to drop the policy. That means all the premiums already paid are, in effect, wasted money.

Fortunately, today people may choose from some more attractive solutions to dealing with the issue of how best to protect assets for the benefit of a spouse and family in the event of a catastrophic illness. One way is, once again, through life insurance. Today, companies offer life insurance policies that provide accelerated benefit riders for long-term care, for chronic illness, or for both. For example, a company may allow anywhere from 40 percent up to 96 percent of a death benefit to be paid out during a policyholder's lifetime to be used to fund his or her long-term-care expenditures. This is an attractive option for all those concerned with the possibility that their premiums, paid for years into a traditional, long-term-care insurance policy, may be lost either because the need for long-term care does not materialize or because their rates are raised so dramatically they are forced to drop the policy.

If someone takes out a life insurance policy with an accelerated benefit rider in order to deal with the issue of long-term care, and if that person does not draw on the policy before passing away, then the life insurance policy pays out an income-tax-free death benefit to the policy beneficiaries. While life insurance proceeds are free of income tax when paid out, they are not always free of estate tax. If the policy owner was the person who passed away, for example, the IRS code brings the death-benefits figure back into the estate for purposes of estate-tax calculation. This is another reason why it is often very desirable to use a life insurance trust specifically to hold the title to a life insurance policy; this way, the proceeds are free of both income and estate tax. Keep in mind that there is no estate tax between spouses.

Another way of dealing with the issue of catastrophic illness is through a single-deposit or single-premium type of a combination of life insurance and a long-term-care life insurance policy. Today, many people keep money in low-yielding money market accounts as emergency funds. However, the emergency most likely to affect a retiree later in life may be the emergency of a catastrophic illness. Suppose catastrophic illness strikes someone who has $100,000 sitting in a money market account. Those money market funds would be spent, dollar for dollar, on healthcare.

Now, suppose we have a sixty-five-year-old female who has $100,000 in a money market account, which she has set aside as a rainy-day or emergency fund. Suppose she takes that $100,000 and puts it into a single-premium or a single-deposit combination life/long-term-care policy. She could experience several benefits as a result of that decision. First, this type of plan typically has a 100-percent money-back guarantee. If, for any reason, at any time, something off the radar happened, the policy holder could say, "Guess what? I need my $100,000 back." That $100,000 would come back to the client with no questions asked and no penalties incurred. Second, if that client never uses the plan for home healthcare, assisted living, or long-term care, she will leave behind an income-tax death benefit that will be paid out to the named beneficiary of her policy upon her death. Third, if she were to suffer a catastrophic illness and need care at home, in an assisted-living facility, or in a nursing home, she would have, on average, about 3 to 4 times the amount of money paid in premiums available for her care. In other words, depending on age, that single, one-time premium payment of $100,000 could create more than $350,000 or $400,000 in a pool of money that would be available to pay for long-term care. Moreover, people can often set up policies whereby they can pay for long-term care over a six- or seven-year period.

Many solutions exist in response to the problems of paying for long-term care. Most likely, a strategy exists that is appropriate for you, but no strategy is any good to you if you do not know your options. To put it simply, you do not know what you do not know. The purpose of meeting with a qualified financial adviser who knows about these topics is to become informed about which solutions are available to you that you may not have considered or of which you were unaware.

One of my clients put money into a single-premium, long-term-care plan. This particular client ended up getting involved in a rather serious automobile accident; he needed months of rehabilitation care and subsequent home healthcare. He and his wife were happy that they had purchased their plan because the plan did what it was supposed to do and covered the costs for them.

Over the years, I have had many clients who have purchased some type of long-term-care protection. Generally, they make such a purchase with a certain amount of reluctance. However, those same clients, clients who end up incurring claims later in life, look back and say, "Well, that was the smartest financial decision I ever made. I preserved the value of all my other assets for the benefit of my spouse and children." On the one hand, purchasing such insurance is not a fun thing to do; on the other hand, it can be a smart thing to do.

Today's world seems to get more and more complicated; as a result, knowledge gets more and more specialized. When I was a kid, we had a family doctor who actually made house calls. Today, it seems that almost every doctor is a specialist. Even attorneys are specialists now. When you are dealing with estate planning, you want to deal with an attorney who specializes in that area. Similarly, when it comes to your financial and retirement-income planning, it is not a smart decision to work with a planner who is a financial generalist and who deals with people of all ages. Generally, you want to work with a person who focuses on retirees and pre-retirees – a person who knows the concerns and objectives that retirees and pre-retirees have regarding retirement-income planning, possible catastrophic illness, current tax minimization planning, and maximizing the value of assets. He or she should help you be able to pass your assets in the most tax-efficient way possible to your family, whether it goes to children, grandchildren or both.

CHAPTER THREE

Could Your Spouse Weather the Worst?

As odd as it sounds, many people are willing to spend a great deal of time and effort planning vacations, but they end up spending far less time and effort planning for their finances in retirement. Even when they do plan for retirement, they may ignore a large *blind spot*. What do I mean by blind spot? Suppose you are driving down the highway and you want to change lanes. You put your turn signal on. You check your mirrors and begin to move into the next lane. All of a sudden, somebody leans on his horn, right next to you. You veer right back into your lane. Afterward, your startled spouse might ask you what happened, and you would explain, "I didn't even see that car. It was in my blind spot." A huge blind spot that can impact couples in retirement, particularly women, is not planning for the likelihood of the husband passing away first. This is a blind spot because, quite frankly, often people just do not want to think about that happening.

Common statistics show that men tend to pass away first and that women, on average, tend to outlive their husbands by about seven years. Anybody who has attended a meeting of seniors, a bingo get-together, or an AARP meeting can relate to this. Almost invariably, more women are present at those meetings, and that reflects the statistical reality that men tend to pass away first. In order to avoid that blind spot, retirees and pre-retirees need to ask, "What's the financial consequence to the surviving spouse in the event that the husband passes away first?"

The first thing that happens is that, suddenly, only one Social Security check is coming in. In the event that the husband passes away first, the government will not continue paying out two Social Security checks to the surviving spouse. One piece of good news is that the surviving spouse will receive the larger of the two Social Security checks; however, the smaller of the two Social Security checks will be gone. Depending upon the check's size, its disappearance may mean an income loss of $1,000 a month or more. Thus, the first topic for retirees and pre-retirees to contemplate is this: "What if you still have to pay your monthly bills but you have $1,000 less each month? Would that impact your lifestyle?"

Often, a reduction in pension payments is even more problematic. For example, this scenario occurs frequently among couples: the husband's pension check is larger than the wife's. Perhaps the husband had a job that paid a higher salary than the wife's job did. Maybe the wife stayed home to raise the children. Maybe she reentered the workforce after the children went to college and, for whatever reason, ended up with no pension or a very small one. More often than not, the husband has a larger pension check.

Often, a husband and wife quickly forget the choices they made regarding that pension when the husband retired. For example, the husband can make a choice about payout rates. He can choose a *life-only pension*, in which case the payments would completely stop upon his passing; in other words, he could choose to have no *survivor benefits*. He could choose a survivor benefit to equal his pension; however, if he makes that choice, the amount of the pension may drop dramatically, often by $1,000 a month or more. Alternatively, he could choose a survivor benefit for the surviving spouse; often, this compromise will protect the wife while preserving a higher monthly pension check during the husband's life. It is common to choose a survivor benefit that may leave 50 percent of the monthly check to the surviving spouse.

A few years ago, I worked with a couple named Fred and Maria. They had chosen this third option several years before I met them. When Fred died, unexpectedly, of a heart attack at age seventy-seven, Maria was unaware that the pension option he had chosen twelve years earlier provided only 50 percent to the survivor. His pension had been $36,000 a year, so awarding 50 percent to the survivor meant that the pension passed along to her was reduced to $18,000 per year. Consider that this comes out to $1,500 a month less in income. The loss of the smaller of the couple's two Social Security payments meant Maria's income was down by another $1,000 a month. After her husband's passing, Maria had $2,500 less per month coming in for the rest of her life.

Maria was three years younger than Fred. At age seventy-four and in good health, she still had many years of life ahead of her. A monthly loss of $2,500 works out to a loss of $30,000 a year. This enormous difference in her finances obliged Maria to sell the family home where she and Fred had lived for forty-plus years, where they had raised their children, and where so many of her happiest memories had been made. After selling the family home, she had to move to an apartment because she needed to invest the proceeds from the sale of the home to make up part of the deficiency caused by the loss of funds caused by her husband's death. This was not a happy option for her; unfortunately, because of a lack of proper planning, it was the only option she had.

Additionally, Maria was forced to drop the long-term-care insurance policy she and Fred had carried because she felt she could no longer afford the payments. If her health failed when she was in her eighties, she would not be able to get assistance from Medicaid to pay nursing-home expenses until she had spent all of her assets and only had $2,000 left. Fred and Maria's example shows how not doing proper planning in this area can result in the unintended consequence of impoverishing the surviving spouse; to make matters worse, it can also result in the unintended consequence of not leaving a legacy to children and grandchildren in the event that the surviving spouse's health should fail later in life.

This is a real problem. This problem affects couples and families across the country on a daily basis, and the media outlets do not focus on it enough. Our society does not adequately acknowledge the problem, but clearly it needs to be addressed. As individuals, we must determine how we can plan ahead to keep this from happening to us.

In a perfect world, each retiree's pension would provide a 100-percent survivor benefit to his or her surviving spouse; unfortunately, the world does not work that way. In fact, the trend in our society is toward a pensionless society. Fewer and fewer companies are offering traditional pensions, and more and more companies are offering 401(k) plans exclusively. As a result of the latter, employees retire with a lump sum of money, and it becomes their responsibility to make sure that money lasts for a lifetime.

What can be done about this situation? The first step is making the right choices relating to a 401(k) account or IRA rollover. Doing so brings up the question of how much risk people should be taking on in retirement and how much money they should leave directly exposed to market fluctuations and risk. People who believe they cannot afford to lose any money in retirement will want to make more conservative choices with the 401(k) account or IRA rollover.

People today often overlook the use of a fixed annuity for part of the 401(k) account or IRA rollover as a solution to this problem. One benefit of using certain types of fixed annuities is the annuities provide a guaranteed rate of growth designed to help meet future income needs of the husband and/or the surviving spouse.

A few weeks ago, a couple named Tom and June came into my office to discuss this very issue. Tom is ten years older than June, who comes from a family in which the women are remarkably long-lived; she has two aunts who are in their nineties, and her mother passed away at age eighty-nine. As a result, in trying to make sure that June would not be impoverished later in life, we looked to a fixed annuity that offered index-linked interest and a guaranteed lifetime-income benefit rider.

The advantage of this type of annuity is the possibility that if its interest rate can be linked to a market index, it may earn more than the interest earned on traditional fixed annuities would earn. More importantly, the particular class of annuities we examined offered guaranteed lifetime-income benefit riders; thus, regardless of the actual amount of interest earned on the underlying annuity, the annuity provider does a calculation to compound the annuity's value for purposes of guaranteeing specific levels of lifetime income. This compounding can be guaranteed at rates of 6, 6.5, or even 7 percent each year.

For example, if somebody has a lifetime-income benefit rider that is compounding at 6 percent per year and he or she makes no withdrawals from the account, in twelve years that person will have available double the initial amount he or she placed in the annuity, from which he or she can take lifetime income withdrawals. The end result of using such an annuity is that a financial planner can design a plan whereby, in the event the husband passes away first and the surviving spouse's income is reduced (due to loss of pension and Social Security payments), an asset is positioned to guarantee a high level of lifetime income that will help replace the lost income.

Moreover, beyond the financial security it provides to a widow, this type of planning can provide a couple with a tremendous benefit: peace of mind. This is particularly true for a husband who might think, "Well, I've been a good provider for my wife and children my entire adult life. Why should that stop in the event of my untimely death?"

Another often-overlooked solution is to take out a life insurance policy on the husband. That used to be the norm, but, unfortunately, the media has biased many people against life insurance. In fact, most articles published in the media will say something to this effect: "You should buy the least expensive term insurance policy you can get; you should only own this when you are young, you still have a mortgage on your house, and your children's education is unfunded. Then, later in life, once your children are educated and your mortgage is paid off, you can get rid of the life insurance because it is an unnecessary expense."

What is overlooked is that retirees often need permanent life insurance. Sometimes, for affluent retirees, this necessitates funding an estate-tax liability or a post-death Roth conversion (discussed in more detail in a subsequent chapter). However, consider this: if a husband had chosen a higher payout on his pension and had taken some of the money from that higher payout to fund a life insurance policy that offered guaranteed premiums and a guaranteed death benefit when he passed away, then hundreds of thousands of dollars in life insurance proceeds could pass to the surviving spouse, free of income tax, and help assure her financial security.

As a result, when June and Fred looked at this issue, they thought, "It makes sense to solve some of this income-replacement issue beyond using the annuity. Why not have a higher payout on the pension and maximize the amount of money available to the surviving spouse by shifting some of that higher payout into a life insurance policy?" That concept is sometimes referred to as *pension maximization* because it can allow a couple to enjoy a higher pension payout during the husband's lifetime while also creating a lump sum to be paid out upon the husband's death.

What happens in this scenario in the event that the wife passes away first? Ultimately, when the husband passes away, the permanent life insurance policy leaves a greater legacy to the beneficiaries.

My former client Tony completed this very plan. He chose a pension payout that would provide him with $8,000 more in annual income. Then, he took $4,000 of that annual increase and purchased a permanent life insurance policy. Now, when he purchased that life insurance policy, Tony never imagined he would come down with Lou Gehrig's disease and pass away in an untimely manner. When that unfortunate event took place, the insurance company paid out $300,000 to his widow, Ann, from which she is able to draw income.

None of us get out of this life alive. None of us like to face the reality of our own mortality or a possible future disability, but facing reality is a wise thing to do. Had she and Tony not made the decision to address the issue, Ann would not be living the comfortable lifestyle that she now enjoys in retirement.

What if the unthinkable, such as a stroke or Alzheimer's disease, happens to you? You can do all the right planning from both a tax and an investment perspective. You can address the issue of one spouse's premature death and meeting the surviving spouse's income needs. However, another pitfall that people often overlook when doing their retirement planning is the possibility of a catastrophic illness occurring later in life. How can financial planners best protect the assets for the benefit of the surviving spouse and family in the event that such an illness should occur?

I can relate to this issue better than most folks because a close family friend of mine was diagnosed with Alzheimer's at age seventy. She passed away at seventy-six as a result of that disease and after spending the last seven months of her life in a convalescent care facility, in a unit that specialized in Alzheimer's patients. This is something that I would not wish on anybody. Alzheimer's is a terrible disease: a loved one slips away while he or she is still physically present. Toward the end, my family friend did not recognize me, any of her friends, or anybody in her family.

Sadly, no cure yet exists for Alzheimer's. However, people can plan for the financial consequences of this disease ahead of the illness. No people know when their time will be up or whether they are going to suffer a stroke or develop Alzheimer's or some other debilitating condition. There are all kinds of statistics relating to long-term care. One states the majority of seniors will need some type of long-term care at some point in life.

So, what can people do to prevent financial devastation in such a scenario? One solution is to look at traditional long-term-care insurance, which is only implemented by 5 percent of the retired population. I think that number may be even smaller in the future. The reason for this low number of people having traditional long-term-care insurance is that the premiums can run into thousands of dollars per year, which few can comfortably afford. Some people weigh their options and make a choice: "It is more important to us to live the lifestyle that we want to live in retirement. Why must we be paying for long-term care insurance that we may never use if it means we can't afford to go to dinner, go to the movies, or take a vacation?"

I think, too, that part of the hesitation to invest in long-term-care insurance is a denial of the possibility that needing such insurance could actually happen. One client told me, "Gee, nobody in my family ever spent time in a nursing home, and nobody on my bowling team ever spent time in a nursing home, so I just didn't think it could happen to me." Sometimes people think their children will care for them, just as those people cared for their parents. They do not think about the fact that many of today's young people live in two-income households. When both partners have to work, it may not be practical or even possible for an adult son or daughter to stay home and care for an ailing parent. This lack of a solution means a return to the problem.

Adding to the problems with traditional long-term-care insurance is the fact that the premiums are not guaranteed. People can take out long-term-care insurance in their mid-sixties and find that it is affordable at that point in time; however, ten years later they can be surprised by rate increases of 20, 30, or 40 percent or more. The reason for such increases is that the actuaries who initially priced the long-term-care insurance got it wrong. They underestimated the actual utilization of long-term-care services. When representatives of a long-term-care insurance company go into the state capital to say to the regulators, "Look, here's what our actual claims experience has been. We need this premium increase," the regulators generally grant them the increase. Obviously, this poses a potential problem for the policyholders who get this large rate increase. Can they afford it? Sometimes the answer is yes, and sometimes the answer is no. What happens if a couple can afford the long-term-care insurance initially, but cannot later on (for example, when the husband passes away and income to the surviving spouse is reduced)? What happens when a surviving spouse is hit with that 30 or 40 percent premium increase for long-term care? She may be forced to drop the coverage and lose all those premiums without getting any benefits.

Clearly, looking at other alternatives is worthwhile. One type of coverage is known as a *single-deposit* or *single-premium* type of long-term care. This generally combines a life insurance death benefit with long-term-care protection. The better plans will have a 100-percent money-back guarantee. How does this work? Suppose a sixty-five-year-old has $100,000 sitting in a money market account or bank CD, earmarked as emergency money. Think about emergencies that can impact an older person: catastrophic illness is certainly one. That sixty-five-year-old could take her $100,000 and put it into a single-deposit or single-premium long-term-care policy, thereby creating a pool of money in excess of $400,000 that would be available to pay for home healthcare, long-term care, assisted living, or nursing-home care. Now, if this individual never used that policy for long-term care, a death benefit would be paid out to the surviving spouse, children, or other beneficiaries of the policy, and it would be free of income tax.

Another scenario plays out when something completely off the radar happens. Suppose this same individual's policy has been in force for 6 months, a year or two, or 36 months, when she says, "Hey, I didn't think I would need this money back. Guess what? I do."

At that point, 100 percent of the premiums can be refunded at no penalty. So, at all times, the money is completely liquid and available for any reason. This solution may be right for some, provided they have liquid money available for the premium payment.

Another solution that can be beneficial is, once again, that of the life insurance policy. This is because of *accelerated benefit riders or chronic illness accelerated benefit riders*. One example of these riders at work can be found in a life insurance policy that would allow acceleration of up to 96 percent of the death benefit over a four-year period to be paid out for long-term care. The funds, which can be paid out prior to the death of the insured, can be used to help pay for long-term care, thereby preserving all of the insured's other assets. People tend to forget that long-term-care benefits under Medicare are limited. Medicare will cover the first 20 days of a nursing-home stay, for example, as long as there is a 3-day prior hospital stay, and as long as the patient requires a skilled level of care. If only an intermediate or a custodial level of care is required, Medicare will not pay anything. Medicare will partially pay for days 21 through 100, but, once again, the patient must have had a 3-day hospital stay and require care at a skilled level. Such requirements are why the expenses of catastrophic illness can be so high. If Medicare partially pays for days 21 through 100, a patient's Medicare supplement policy may also partially pay for days 21 through 100. After that, the patient is on his or her own. Payments of $200 or more for each day spent in a long-term-care facility can really add up.

Another option to consider is an annuity program that includes a *confinement rider* or a *long-term-care rider*. This can provide a dramatic increase in income when it may be needed most. Again, I cannot stress enough the importance of consulting with a knowledgeable adviser who is trained to find a plan that is best for you. My bigger point is that you must *plan*. If you plan for the worst and hope for the best, you could be safe and secure, no matter what curveballs life may throw your way.

CHAPTER FOUR

(Almost) Everything You Need to Know about IRAs

W hy the *almost* in this chapter's title? Put it this way: Everything you need to know about IRAs could fill a multi-volume treatise, because IRAs are complicated. While many rules relate to IRAs, my intention in this chapter is to hit some of the most important areas of IRAs in which most people need to be more financially literate in order to make smart choices.

IRAs are potentially hostile assets as far as taxes are concerned. In fact, I sometimes refer to IRAs as "tax-infested accounts." That may seem contrary to what most people have learned over the years regarding the tax advantages of IRAs, 401(k) accounts, 403(b) accounts, 457 plans, and employer-sponsored, tax-deferred plans in general. People have been taught they should sock away as much money as they possibly can in IRAs, 401(k) accounts, and other employer-sponsored plans, the theory being the more money people grow on a tax-deferred basis, the better off they are. This makes sense, but what people have assumed in this equation is that when they take the money out in retirement, they will be in a much lower tax bracket, which is not necessarily the case. What my colleagues and I find with our clients when they begin taking out retirement income is that many are either in the same tax bracket they were in when they were working or they are one tax bracket lower. Often, the requirement of minimum distributions, which the government forces on people in their seventies, can push retirees back up into the same tax bracket they were in while working. Taking those distributions can have very unpleasant tax consequences, too.

For example, let me tell the story of a client named Sally, who was in her sixties when I began working with her. She needed to buy a new car. Without talking to me first, she took $28,000 out of her IRA and used that to buy the car. Unfortunately, that withdrawal resulted in the IRA company sending her a 1099 form, and she had to pay tax on $28,000 of additional income. As it happened, she also had about $50,000 sitting in a money market account when she made that IRA withdrawal. Had she used $28,000 of her after-tax dollars in the money market account, her car purchase would have had no negative tax consequence.

Generally, people in their sixties tend to have separate piles of money, so to speak: first, the after-tax money, or money that is outside their retirement accounts; second, the money in their retirement accounts. They tend to use the money outside their retirement accounts first because they do not want to generate additional taxable income by pulling money out of IRAs or 401(k) accounts. In such a case, the IRA continues to grow on a tax-deferred basis and can become a tax time-bomb, particularly if the money is left in an employer's sponsored plan. I could tell several horror stories about people who left money in employer-sponsored plans, such as 401(k) plans, rather than upgrade or move that money to their own IRAs. How can people best utilize those retirement savings and avoid creating a tax bomb in so doing? The solution lies in proper planning.

Leaving money in an employer-sponsored plan can be a disastrous decision. A journalist writing for a Sunday newspaper reported a story about an employer who did not maintain his 401(k) plan documents the way they were supposed to be. The company ended up filing for bankruptcy and the government froze the plan assets; even four years later, none of the employees were able to withdraw any money.

People have different types of planning that have to be done relating to IRAs. One type has to do with where to put the IRA – in other words, the choice of vehicles in which the IRA money should be positioned. The other type has to do with taxes. In this chapter, I focus on tax planning related to IRAs and qualified retirement plans. In the next chapter, I deal more specifically with where people should perhaps put IRAs.

First, I want to focus on the genesis of IRAs and 401(k) accounts. Why do they exist? Prior to the 1970s, people did not really have 401(k) accounts or IRAs. Retirement planning for most people was relatively simple because so many of retirees received traditional pension checks. All they had to do was shop for the highest CD rates into which they could put their retirement savings. It was not very complicated to compare CD rates then, and interest rates were much higher years ago than they are today.

In the 1970s, representatives of American corporations woke up to the fact that people were living longer, and they began to lobby the government to establish an alternative system of funding retirement: they wanted to get the financial liability of paying pensions for twenty to thirty years off their books. What the politicians and the corporate representatives came up with were the 401(k) account and IRA systems. The idea was to give employees certain tax breaks when they contributed money to a 401(k) account or an IRA while encouraging corporations to match the money in some way. Theoretically, this combination would create a huge, tax-deferred nest egg for each retiree to draw on in retirement. Sometimes this combination works out that way, and sometimes it does not.

Initially, the issues relating to this topic revolve around the question of what an individual should do if he or she has left a 401(k) account in a former employer's 401(k) holdings. Is that a wise thing to do? Most of the time, no; it is generally not a wise thing to do. That is because when people leave money in a former employer's 401(k) account, their investment choices are limited to the offerings that the employer makes available in that 401(k). Often, those options are minimal. When an individual elects to do a tax-free rollover from a 401(k) account to an IRA, a much broader choice of investments become available to him or her. Thus, one reason to roll over an employer-sponsored plan to an IRA is that more choices regarding the positioning of the money become available.

Another reason to roll over the money to an IRA concerns multigenerational planning. For example, often an employer's 401(k) plan was drafted many years ago and calls for a lump-sum distribution of the 401(k) account upon the account-holder's death to non-spousal beneficiaries. Suppose a wife predeceases her husband. His 401(k) account then goes to an adult son or daughter.

Harry and Margaret were prospective clients of my firm who struggled with this decision. For whatever reason, they were procrastinators and did not make the right decisions to move forward with proper planning. Some time after meeting with them, I heard from good friends of theirs, who were also clients of mine, that Margaret had passed away. Two years later, when Harry passed away, the couple's daughter, Susan, contacted the 401(k) company to file a death claim. Apparently, she spoke with a girl in her early twenties who said, "I can help you with this claim. I can even populate the claim form and mail it out to you for your signature."

To make a long story short, this happened. Susan, who was grieving the loss of her father, simply signed the form and sent it back in. The company generated a lump-sum check and withheld a 20-percent tax; the opportunity to continue tax deferral on this money was lost. That would not have happened had that 401(k) account been rolled over properly to an IRA, and had Harry and Margaret been committed to working with a qualified adviser who understood the concept of multigenerational distribution planning as it relates to IRAs. That mess could have been averted.

The whole idea is this: an individual can set up an IRA during his or her lifetime so that he or she is able to take income distributions as needed. If, for example, all he or she wants to do is take the required minimum distributions, he or she can do that; in contrast, if that individual has a greater need for income, he or she can withdraw more. When an account passes, at the death of the first spouse, to the surviving spouse, the surviving spouse gets to continue receiving income from the IRA. However, in order for that account to pass properly and continue tax deferral to the next generation, it must be properly set up as an inherited IRA.

When the account becomes an inherited IRA, it is retitled. If you, for instance, are the deceased account holder, the title would read as follows: your name, deceased, IRA F.B.O. (for benefit of), and the name of your ultimate beneficiary. The stipulation for such an arrangement is that the IRA beneficiary has to take the required minimum distribution each year for a number of years, and that number is based upon the beneficiary's life expectancy. For example, beneficiaries in their seventies or eighties have to take out much larger required distribution from an IRA than that required of beneficiaries in their forties or fifties. One reason that 401(k) accounts, 403(b) accounts, 457 plans, and deferred compensation plans often grow into 6 or sometimes 7 figures is because one-third of the earnings generated do not have to be given each year to the government (in the form of current taxes) as money accumulates within the plan. Obviously, it can be desirable for a family to continue IRA tax deferral across multiple generations and across the lifetimes of children or even grandchildren.

The message here is this: If you have left money in employer-sponsored plans, such as 401(k) accounts, 403(b) accounts, 457 plans, or deferred compensation plans, why not consider consolidating these accounts into an IRA with multigenerational distribution planning in mind?

First, look at setting up your IRA with the maximum tax advantages for you and your family. This brings up the question of what a Roth conversion is and whether it is preferable to convert traditional IRA money to a Roth IRA. Every dollar that comes out of a traditional IRA is subject to income taxes, no matter who takes the money out. If you believe income-tax rates are likely to be higher in the future than they are today (perhaps because of the government's lack of fiscal responsibility), you might be better off with a Roth IRA, since the money in a Roth IRA grows free of income-tax. When it is distributed, it remains free of income tax. While a Roth IRA has to be in existence for five years before the income distributions are tax-free, most people plan on holding a Roth more than five years before taking income distributions.

"Okay," you might be thinking, "I've got $400,000 or $500,000 in this traditional IRA. How would I go about converting that to a tax-free Roth IRA?" Most corporate custodians of IRAs offer forms that can be filled out for Roth conversions. The consequence of doing this, however, is that a *conversion tax* will be incurred. This is an income tax that has to be paid on the amount being converted. If you convert a $400,000 or $500,000 traditional IRA to a Roth, the tax bite will be substantial. The bite could bump you up to a maximum federal tax bracket (35 percent in 2012). As of 2013, the rate is scheduled to be 39.6 percent. If you pay state income tax, you could end up paying in the neighborhood of 8 percent or more state income tax on the amount being converted in addition to the federal income tax.

You are probably thinking, "If I have to pay a federal tax rate of 39.6 percent and a state tax rate of 8 percent, I'll be giving up 47.6 percent of the account just to turn it into a Roth IRA." That is why many retirees determine that it does not make sense for them to do this conversion, since they think it would take them too long to recoup the cost of the conversion. Oddly enough, however, many people will leave an IRA exposed to excessive direct market fluctuation and risk, and they may end up facing a loss similar in cost to what the conversion taxes might have cost.

Often, the smarter move is to do the post-death or postmortem Roth conversion. Suppose a seventy-year-old couple decides not to do the Roth conversion because they do not like the idea of giving up more than 40 percent of the account to the tax man. Since they do not need all of the required minimum distribution monies to pay their bills, they take the required minimum distribution funds and shift that money into life insurance by using an insurance trust. By doing so, they can create a pool of money that will be available upon their passing and allow their children to do a post-death Roth conversion.

A post-death Roth conversion can be structured in a number of different ways. Sometimes a couple may feel it is desirable to convert an account to a Roth upon the death of the first spouse; in such a case, they place the life insurance death benefit upon the husband, and the payout is generated upon his passing. The conversion can then be done at that point in time.

As long as a Roth account has been in existence for five years, withdrawals taken out of it are not subject to the same five-year waiting period they would be subject to if no Roth IRA existed. That is why it is often a wise planning move to have a small amount of money in a Roth IRA, especially if the expectation is that a larger sum of money may be added down the road through a conversion.

The main idea here is that you should look at what you are trying to accomplish with your IRA or IRAs. Are you trying to avoid long-term taxation? Are you trying to continue tax deferral across multiple generations? Are you interested in transforming a tax-infested, traditional IRA into a tax-free IRA in a cost-effective manner? What is important to you about your money?

These are the questions that a good financial adviser is going to ask you about your attitude toward your retirement account. All too often, historic decisions relating to retirement plan accounts have focused on how to invest the money in the account rather than how to draw money from the account in the most tax-efficient way. Normally, the most tax-efficient way is to take the money out over a specific period of time so that it can be taxed at a lower rate than it would be if it were drawn out all at once.

Making smart choices relating to positioning a retirement plan account matters. However, even with the best tax planning in the world, if an individual leaves a retirement account exposed to excessive risk, he or she may have accomplished very little if he or she loses that money to adverse market conditions. Retirees face two big threats relating to their retirement savings. The first threat, of course, has to do with excessive taxation and can be addressed by proper planning. The second has to do with investment risk, which can also be addressed through proper planning. (More details can be found in the next chapter).

I cannot overstress how important it is to work with a knowledgeable adviser who is up-to-date on the rules relating to IRAs. One of my clients told me how the son of his good friend Larry had inadvertently triggered taxation on the entire IRA balance his father was leaving to him. Notably, Larry had happened to attend a lecture I gave. During this lecture, I talked about multigenerational distribution planning and how an IRA, when set up properly, can be stretched over the lifetime of the next generation. Larry subsequently had a conversation with his son and told him, "You know, if anything ever happens to me, you can take this IRA and stretch it out over your life expectancy. You do not have to pay lump-sum income taxation on it."

Five years later, when Larry passed away, his son John remembered this conversation while taking the IRA proceeds he had inherited from his father. Based on what his dad had told him, John thought he could stretch it over his lifetime. Unfortunately, John made the mistake of comingling it with his own IRA money. When he added the inherited money to his own IRA, instead of a properly titled inherited IRA, John triggered lump-sum income taxation on the entire amount he had inherited, which was substantial; in addition, he had to pay a 6-percent penalty tax.

The message, once again, is that there are certain areas in which it is perfectly fine to be a do-it-yourselfer, and others in which the do-it-yourself approach can be foolhardy. For instance, I have a passion for gardening, and I like being a do-it-yourselfer when it comes to the backyard; however, if I needed dental work or surgery, I would not be a do-it-yourselfer. I think the mistake that too many people make today is they want to be do-it-yourselfers when it comes to their retirement planning. However, the consequence of that is that things can get botched, and those mistakes can cost families hundreds of thousands of dollars in unnecessary taxes that could have been avoided through proper planning.

CHAPTER FIVE

Get Off the Roller Coaster

Will Rogers is credited with saying he was concerned more about the return *of* his principal than the return *on* his principal. Of course, most people should try to avoid losing money, particularly money needed to produce income in retirement. Despite this fact, many people position their retirement savings as if they were still in the 1990s. Why? I think it is because their frame of reference is based on their past experience.

For example, those who started investing in mutual funds in the late 1970s or early 1980s and kept investing in mutual funds throughout the twenty-year period of the 1980s and 1990s might have been led to conclude from their earnings that, even with brief interruptions, the stock market always seemed to go up. Many of the financial magazines of the 1990s promoted the view that all people needed to do was put money into low-expense index mutual funds because returns were then very high. According to articles in those magazines, investors did not need a financial adviser; they could do everything on their own. Certainly, in the 1990s, the performance of the S&P 500 was very impressive.

However, an examination of the years 2000 to 2010, and even 2011, reveals a very different conclusion. Many people tell me they are frustrated because they feel their money has been on a roller-coaster ride for the last eleven or twelve years. I remember one individual, Harry, and his wife, Nancy, from when they first came into my office. When I asked them what their concerns were, they dropped their IRA statement on my desk. A major brokerage firm had managed their IRA for the previous twelve years, largely investing the money in a *mutual fund wrap program* (a program in which mutual funds are wrapped together). Their broker at the brokerage firm charged them an additional fee for managing the mutual funds. Harry was frustrated because he had not made any money over the previous ten years. His experience, like that of many others, was that his account had grown tremendously in the 1990s, when the market was more or less consistently going up. Then, when the dot-com bubble burst and the thirty-one-month bear market endured from 2000 to 2003, he watched a substantial portion of his retirement savings evaporate. All through it, his broker reassured him: "Don't worry, this is temporary. The market always comes back. You don't want to sell at a loss right now. It's only a paper loss." So, he stayed the course. Sure enough, he saw his account rebound from 2003 through 2007, only to have the losses happen all over again during the financial crisis of 2008 to 2009.

At the time of our meeting, Harry felt strongly that he could not afford to keep riding this financial rollercoaster, particularly now that he was approaching the point at which he needed to draw a dependable, predictable income from his retirement savings. Adding to his concern was an article he had read that questioned the validity of what financial advisers call the *4-percent rule*; the brief definition of this rule is that if a retiree has a properly balanced portfolio – namely, a mix of stocks and bonds – he or she should be able to withdraw at a 4-percent rate without worrying about running out of money before his or her life ends, likely somewhere in the mid- to late-eighties. The article's author suggested that rule might no longer be valid because of increased volatility in the stock market and poor yields in the bond market. The frustration that many retirees like Harry feel builds up because they are uncertain where to turn. Where should they go if they leave the market? How should they best position their retirement savings, particularly the portion needed to produce an income that must be there, no matter what?

The costs of not getting off the roller coaster are much more difficult than the difficulties posed by finding creative solutions, however. At the very beginning of 2000, a prospective client came in to my firm. He told me that when he was about to retire, he had a fairly substantial IRA and a 401(k) account that he had heavily invested in individual stocks, particularly technology and dot-com stocks. At our meeting, I suggested he think about diversifying and consider positioning some of his portfolio more conservatively. During our conversation, he told me he felt he should be guaranteed a 10-percent return per year on his portfolio because, after all, that is what the stock market had been doing in the 1990s. He felt any financial professional should be able to deliver this return to him.

I pointed out that this was not a realistic expectation; the fact the market had done well in the 1990s was no reason to expect it would continue to do well, and many people felt the market was overvalued at its current level and was due for a major correction. This was not what he wanted to hear. He ended up not becoming a client.

A few years later, I happened to be shopping in the local Home Depot and ran into him. He had on an orange vest and his belt held a tape measure. Clearly, he was working there.

I asked him, "Gee, what made you decide to work at the Home Depot?"

He said, "Well, I'm not really working here because I want to work here. I'm working here because I have to work here. I hate to say it, but I should have listened to you."

While it was gratifying to know I had given the right advice, it was sad that this man hadn't taken my advice. What I saw there was how making bad financial decisions can have real consequences in a person's life. Since that encounter, whenever I see elderly people working at McDonald's, Wal-Mart, or Lowe's or the Home Depot, I always wonder whether they are there because they want to be there or because they have to be there. Some people may never retire as a result of not getting the right advice and not making the right financial decisions.

The old answers do not work as they did. For example, look at bank CD rates today. While people generally consider CDs safe, the rate of return on CDs today is abysmally low. Most people would say, "If I position my retirement savings in CDs at these low interest rates, I'm not going to be able to throw off enough interest earnings to meet my income needs, so that's not an effective solution. And if I put too much of my retirement savings in individual stocks, I might make a lot of money or I might lose a lot of money. If I lose a lot of money, I don't have any do-overs in retirement. I can't go back to work and make that money all over again. What about bonds?

Should I just go and put my retirement savings into bonds if I'm not comfortable with the risks of individual stocks?"

The challenge here is that bonds are not free of risk; instead, they are subject to two different risk factors. One risk factor is known as *credit risk*: the risk that the bonds become worthless because the company issuing the bonds runs into credit problems or ends up having to file for bankruptcy. This happened to a gentleman named Tom, who came into my office for a meeting a few years ago. He expressed frustration because his broker had recommended he buy bonds issued by a major U.S. airline. Tom did so, and then that airline filed for bankruptcy. Tom was upset that his bonds, which had once paid an attractive yield, had become worthless. Bonds are subject to credit risk; their health depends on the health of their issuing company.

The other risk to which bonds are subject is known as *interest-rate risk*. An example of this type of risk shows up in an old expression: "When interest rates go up, bonds values go down." Most people have heard that, but many do not understand exactly why that is the case. I like to explain it to clients this way: Say you purchase a bond or put together a bond portfolio today, when rates are at fifty-year lows. Suppose you have a bond that has a ten-year maturity on it and your bond is paying a yield of 4 percent. Suppose, too, that in two, three, or four years from now, for whatever reason, you will need or want to sell that bond. Somebody on the opposite end of the transaction will buy that bond from you. Now, suppose rates were to go up 2 percent. That would mean somebody could buy a new corporate bond paying a 6-percent return. In that case, why would they want to buy your bond at 4 percent? The answer is they would not buy your bond, unless you were willing to discount it or sell it off at a loss to them so the discount would match the yield they could get on a new bond. Follow this rule of thumb: if a bond has a ten-year duration, for every 1-percent rise in interest rates you can expect to lose 10 percent of the bond's value. If rates go up 2 or 3 percent over the next five years, which many people believe is possible, you stand to lose 20 percent to 30 percent of the value of the bond or bond portfolio. People intuitively know that it is not a good idea to have too much money in bonds when interest rates are so low. Thus, if CDs, stocks, and bonds do not present the total solution, retirees and pre-retirees wonder if there is anything else at which they should be looking or if there is anything they are overlooking.

In fact, there is. I think a good way to describe this alternative is to describe what it does first and then come back to what it is called. I have asked many people the following question: "If the government put us on a committee and said, 'Design the ideal retirement savings vehicle,' what elements might we want to see in that ideal retirement savings vehicle?"

Well, the first thing people will typically say is, "I'd really like to see my account value not go backward. If the stock market is plummeting in value or if the bond market is going down in value, I don't want to be getting statements that show I'm losing money when I can't afford to lose money." In other words, their first criterion might be protection of their principal.

Their second criterion is usually upside earnings potential. People say, "Yes, protecting my principal is important, but I would also like to have the potential to earn a higher rate of interest than I could get in a CD. If all I wanted to do was protect my principal, I could just put my money in CDs and my principal would be protected. Instead, I'd like to earn something on my money at the same time I'm saving it, and I'd like to have some upside potential."

The third criterion, for many people, might be the ability to guarantee a specific level of income for life, or a *lifetime income guarantee*. Ideally, this dream retirement savings vehicle would protect the principal when the market goes down, so that account holders do not have to worry about losing money, but offer the ability, when the market goes up, to help the account holders make money.

Most people would say a proposal like that sounds ideal. However, when you explain to those same people that there are, in fact, certain types of annuities that do all this, many of those people's brains will shut down. Why? The reason is that the media outlets have highlighted some bad annuities out there. As a result, a reasonable person might draw the conclusion that all annuities are bad, but nothing is further from the truth.

For example, suppose the first car you ever bought was a compact car that was manufactured in what was formerly Yugoslavia. Suppose this car had nothing but mechanical problem after problem after problem. If, based on that experience, you drew the conclusion that no cars are any good and you would never want a car again for the rest of your life, you'd be short-changing yourself in a big way. Right? By the same token, if you read an article in a magazine that states some annuities have high fees and expenses, or some annuities have very long surrender charge periods, or some annuities pay the brokers ridiculous commissions, you would be wrong to draw the conclusion that all annuities do those things.

The topic of the next chapter is annuities; in it, you will learn about some of the exciting new options for income security annuities can offer retirees.

CHAPTER SIX

*Millennial Money Smarts:
The New Look
of Annuities*

In the last chapter, I talked about some of the different investment choices that are available to you, including their upsides and downsides. In this chapter, I would like to walk you through the world of annuities.

As I said, many of my clients have expressed doubts whenever the word *annuity* first comes up in a discussion of retirement income vehicles. Generally, annuities have gotten a bad rap in the past for many reasons. The fact is there are different types of annuities, just as there are different types of *automobile*s. If I say the word automobile, one person might picture a Cadillac Escalade. Another person might picture a Toyota Prius. The two imagined cars are both automobiles, but they are very different vehicles.

Sometimes people will say to me, "I was watching television and a commentator said to stay away from variable annuities. Why is that?" The answer is some variable annuities have very high fees and expenses, which can run between 3 and 4 percent per year. If you have a variable annuity with expenses of 3.5 percent per year, you will pay $3,500 a year in fees and expenses for each $100,000 in that variable annuity. Thus, most people conclude that the variable annuities are a little bit too pricey for them. Keep in mind that variable annuities are securities products sold by prospectus and subject to investment risk. Typically, companies offering these products charge additional fees to provide a death benefit guarantee for the beneficiaries or an income guarantee for the account holder.

On the other end of the spectrum from a variable annuity is something known as an *immediate annuity*, with one of these annuities, you trade a lump sum away to an insurance company for a stream of payments, or a pension, guaranteed for life. The problem with immediate annuities is that because interest rates are very low – as of this writing, completed in 2012 – buyers can lock in a low interest or payout rate either for the rest of their lives or for that payout period. Life-only immediate annuities also pose a particular danger: if the account holder passes away prematurely, the payments will stop and the insurance company will keep the money. That is why my colleagues and I do not like life-only immediate annuities.

What my colleagues and I have found to be worth looking at are certain types of fixed annuities. First of all, fixed annuities are generally considered safe for consumers because the insurance companies that issue fixed annuities are part of the legal reserve system. That means the government requires insurance companies that issue fixed annuities to maintain dollar-for-dollar reserves; so, for every dollar they take in in annuities, they have to maintain that amount in reserves to back up those annuities. The insurance companies also have to maintain a capital surplus beyond that amount. I would challenge anybody to find anyone, anywhere, who has lost money in a fixed annuity. (In fact, the only way I know an account holder could lose money in a fixed annuity is to surrender the account early during the surrender charge period, which may incur a surrender charge.) Fixed annuities generally pay higher rates of interest than those offered by banks, and some fixed annuities give account holders the ability to link an account's rate of interest to the performance of different market indexes, such as Standard and Poor's (S&P) 500 Index.

Now, that said, imagine what might happen to you if you link your interest credit in your fixed annuity to the S&P 500 Index. You will not be getting 100 percent of the gain, which you would be getting if you were bearing a risk of loss. This procedure places caps on the account's upside earnings potential. In contrast, if you had money in a mutual fund tied to the S&P 500, and the mutual fund went up substantially, there would be no cap on your upside earnings potential. Yet, if you owned that mutual fund in a year like 2001 or 2008, when the S&P 500 dropped in value substantially, you would lose a big chunk of money. If you use a fixed annuity that offers index-linked interest, your upside earnings will be capped if you link your interest credit to the S&P 500. You might have an annual or a *monthly cap* on the upside earnings, depending on the company and the product; however, if the index goes backward, you will not lose money.

Many people like the fixed annuity that offers index-linked interest because they like the idea of something that gives them the ability to make money when the S&P 500 goes up and avoid losing money when the S&P 500 goes down.

Another very appealing element of this type of annuity is that whatever account holders make, they keep. In a year like 2006 or 2007, in which the S&P 500 finishes the year up, and an account holder has a favorable or positive interest credit as a result, that interest credit becomes part of the account holder's principal, so to speak. Suppose the following year is a year like 2008; the account holder does not have to give back any of the interest that he or she earned in the prior year. What account holders make, they keep. That is attractive to people too.

A recent interesting innovation in this area is a *guaranteed lifetime income benefit rider.* A *rider* is something that gets added on to an annuity. Typically, having this rider, or additional benefit, on an annuity results in an additional expense, or fee. However, what this rider does is guarantee a specific level of income for life. I had somebody in my office a few months ago who had looked at these fixed-index annuities. She had concluded it would be just her luck to take a position in the product and later find that interest rates had remained terribly low or that the market index had done nothing for ten years. She was afraid she would earn very little in the annuity, and she wanted to be assured she would get a fixed level of income.

A guaranteed lifetime income benefit rider can, for example, guarantee a specific rate of growth for the purpose of covering a future income need. For example, suppose one guaranteed lifetime income rider had a growth rate of 7 percent per year; then, what is commonly referred to as the *income account value,* or *benefit base,* of the annuity would increase by 7 percent per year. Now, that increase is not provided for the purpose of the account holder walking away with a lump sum, the way one does at the end of a CD's term. Rather, it is for the purpose of guaranteeing the account holder a specific level of income. Say a guaranteed lifetime income benefit rider had a growth rate of 7.2 percent over the course of ten years and a client started with $100,000 in that annuity. Ten years later, that account holder would have $200,000 in income account value in the annuity.

Now, if he or she then became ready to start taking out income, a specific level of income would be guaranteed to him or her for life. Depending upon the policyholder's age, he or she might be guaranteed 5, 5.5, or 6 percent for life.

Another advantage of this type of annuity is that it does not require any *annuitization* to generate this lifetime income. In the past, if someone wanted to generate a guaranteed lifetime income from an annuity, he or she would have to *annuitize*; in other words, he or she would have to trade his or her lump sum away to the insurance company. The account holder would not own his or her lump sum anymore; he or she would have traded it for a stream of payments. The advantage of the guaranteed lifetime income benefit rider is that an account holder who has such a rider can start an income stream and still have a lump sum in the annuity. If the account holder passes away, that lump sum may become totally liquid for the beneficiary, typically either a surviving spouse or a child.

These annuities are especially helpful in helping to cover retirement's *income gap*, which is defined as the difference between an individual's fixed expenses on a monthly basis and that individual's base income. For example, one of my clients, John, was concerned about making sure he met the income gap. He had Social Security payments of approximately $2,000 per month; he had a pension of $1,000 per month; and his monthly expenses totaled about $4,000 per month. That meant he had a $1,000 per month difference between his income requirements and what his pension and Social Security provided. He wanted to make sure he had that income gap covered, no matter what happened with the stock market, the bond market, or the economy.

I suggested he and I look at a fixed annuity that offered index-linked interest and a guaranteed lifetime income benefit rider.

Sometimes, these types of accounts are termed *hybrid fixed annuities*, since this type of product offers a choice each year between fixed interest and index-linked interest. In contrast, a traditional fixed annuity only offers a fixed rate of interest.

So, John and I looked at a fixed-index annuity to fulfill that income gap. John felt that this type of annuity was an ideal solution for him; having that income gap covered, no matter what, meant he would sleep well at night. He was also pleased that this annuity would give him the freedom to position other retirement savings in other investments. In those cases, he would be willing to take on some risk in exchange for a potentially higher reward. John could afford to take that kind of risk because he knew that if those investments did not work out the way he expected, his income needs would still be met. In situations like his, such annuities can be particularly helpful.

Now, as good as these programs are, people should not go overboard with them. While these programs have very beneficial features, they do have a couple of features that merit a closer look. The first of these features is the *surrender charge schedule*, which puts a limit on the rate at which the account holder can withdraw funds from the account during the first seven or ten years, or sometimes longer. What does that mean? Suppose an annuity has a ten-year term. Typically, during that ten-year term, the account holder can withdraw 10 percent of the entire annuity value each year; however, if the account holder withdraws more than 10 percent, he or she can incur an early withdrawal penalty. The reason account holders do not want to go overboard with withdrawals is to have cash available for emergencies. Thus, these accounts have their place; however, because they have a liquidity restriction, it would be imprudent to put an excessive amount of money into them. Retirees have to have some money available to handle emergencies. Some of today's annuities will allow account holders to walk away with a complete, 100-percent return of the original premium at the end of twenty-four months if they are not absolutely thrilled with the account's performance – and there is no penalty.

The second feature of these accounts that merits examination is that they place caps on the upside earnings potential; as a result, account holders are not going to make 100 percent of the gain that the market index itself makes. Again, where these accounts can be most beneficial is in providing a vehicle that protects a portion of retirement savings against market risks, has upside earnings potential, and guarantees a specific level of income for life. They are certainly worth considering for part of your retirement savings portfolio, and, by helping you to fill the income gap, they can offer you peace of mind.

One of my clients, Bob, is a retired university professor. Bob is a brilliant, published author who has written textbooks used at universities across the country. He is one of the smartest individuals I have ever met; yet, Bob once made the mistake of trusting the wrong person. Bob was dealing with a broker at a major brokerage firm that his accountant had recommended. During the financial meltdown in 2008, Bob lost more than a million dollars. As his portfolio evaporated, his broker kept reassuring him, saying, "Don't worry. It will come back."

When Bob first met with me, at the suggestion of one of his neighbors (another client of mine), he said he wanted something that would not go down in value – something that had some upside potential. We went over his choices. He decided to roll over a portion of his IRA, approximately $500,000, to a fixed-index annuity, and he linked the interest credit to the S&P 500. He opened his account in February 2009, using an interest crediting method called the monthly cap (sometimes referred to as the *monthly point-to-point strategy*). A year later, in February 2010, Bob was pleased to see a double-digit interest credit in his account. Now, I do not want to suggest in any way that fixed-index annuities can return double-digit interest credits every year. That is the exception, not the rule. Bob wanted something that would not go backward; he wanted to know that he would keep what he made. In addition, he wanted something that had a little more upside potential than a CD, a bond, or a traditional fixed annuity. Fixed-index annuities were an ideal solution for him. Needless to say, he and his wife are very happy and pleased with their account's results.

To take Bob's example a step further, think about what might happen if the next twelve-month period turned out to be a bust. Suppose something happens in the world that disrupts the stock market or the economy. For example, say that a major war starts in the Middle East, or a European country defaults on its debt. Suppose that, as a result, the stock market index that Bob had linked his interest credit to goes down 20 percent. Well, in that scenario, Bob would see no interest credit; fortunately, the interest credits he had made in prior years would remain in his annuity. From his perspective, Bob likes the idea that what he makes, he keeps, and he also likes the idea that he will not lose any money in the occasional years in which the indexes go backward. These features are very appealing to many people regardless of whether those people are retired automobile mechanics or university professors.

The message here is that there are alternatives to look at for a portion of retirement savings that do not involve direct stock and bond market risk, and you should consider them. You should start by working with a financial adviser who has knowledge of these programs. Unfortunately, I have found that many financial advisers are not knowledgeable because they are not truly independent. In other words, the firm they work for sets the agenda on what they should be offering or presenting to clients. Many times, the firms these advisers work for do not want to see assets going out the door of the investment house. An adviser in that situation cannot really work objectively for clients; he or she is working for his or her employer.

So far in this book, I have focused on the importance of doing proper estate and tax planning, along with the importance of positioning your money so that it is not subject to excessive estate taxes. I have also gone over protection in the event of a catastrophic illness, as well as protecting some retirement savings against excessive market risk.

In the next chapter, I describe what happens to your money after you are gone. Many folks worry about what is going to happen to their estates and who will benefit. How can your assets best be positioned to serve those you leave behind, and to serve them in the most tax-efficient way? The answer is in wealth transfer planning.

CHAPTER SEVEN

In-Laws, Outlaws, and Predatory Taxes

I work with clients from all points on the spectrum of income and assets. Many of my clients are from the upper middle-class; others have more modest circumstances; and some are very wealthy. Over the years, I have noticed that most of them have one thing in common: whether they are rich or poor, many of them share a concern over who will get their money when they pass away. They love their children, but very often they do not particularly love or trust their children's spouses. They also worry about who will end up with their estates should their children get divorced. They do not want to see their money go into the hands of the divorcing in-laws; they want to keep that money safe for their adult children and grandchildren. They do not want to see that money eaten up in taxes, either.

No retiree, or even pre-retiree, likes facing the reality that probably more life lies behind than ahead. Much of retirement planning consists of the topics covered in this book (particularly retirement income planning and tax minimization planning); however, wealth transfer planning is something that people sometimes do not want to address. In part, this is because many people are concerned about how much money they will need to get through the balance of their life, particularly if their health status should change.

Part of what a good financial planner does is help clients with retirement income planning, not by focusing on meeting the income needs of only the next year or two, but by focusing many years into the future, to the end of their clients' lives or beyond. A good financial planner will also work with clients to put some sort of plan in place to address the possibility of a catastrophic illness occurring later in life. Once you have worked with a good adviser to identify what assets are earmarked or set aside for supplemental income generation to provide income beyond what your pension and Social Security will generate, and once you have got your income gap met and put a plan in place for dealing with the high cost of a catastrophic illness, you can look at your assets and, very possibly, come to the realization that you are probably not going to spend every dime you have accumulated during your lifetime.

Once that light bulb is turned on – "I'm not going to spend every dime I've accumulated" – a second light bulb should be turned on: you cannot take it with you. None of us are getting out of this life alive. The question then becomes, "What happens to the accumulated savings and investments left behind?"

Regarding estate planning, earlier I recommended having an up-to-date will and possibly creating additional documents, such as those dealing with trusts. I want to expand on that here and discuss the possibilities offered to you through legal documents, particularly what those documents can do for you when they are drafted properly and you are working with a team. However, I will not give legal advice in this chapter.

Which individuals should make up your team? Ideally, you are consulting with a qualified financial adviser who works closely with a qualified estate-planning attorney; that attorney, in turn, should work closely with an accountant. When you have a team approach to solving your money challenges in retirement, you are much more likely to have a favorable outcome.

Suppose you have arrived at the point at which you say, "Okay, I've got X amount of dollars. I'm not going to spend it all, and I'm not going to take it all with me. Isn't it enough to have a simple will that spells out that, upon my passing, my estate goes to my surviving spouse, and after that it goes to the children?"

The answer is most likely no, depending on the level of your assets. For example, the federal government has a federal estate tax. Many state governments have state estate taxes. Originally, leaders of the federal government scheduled a $1 million threshold for the federal estate tax to go into effect on January 1, 2013. The threshold did not actually go into effect because of the Fiscal Cliff Bill passed on January 1, 2013. This bill created a threshold of $5,250,000, a number that is indexed for inflation. Of course, subsequent politicians can change the estate tax threshold again in the future simply by changing the law again. How can people predict, with any degree of certainty, what the federal estate-tax threshold will be at the end of life, particularly if that is fifteen to twenty-five years in the future? The answer, obviously, is that people cannot predict. Each person can only do the best he or she can in terms of planning ahead to deal with whatever the government throws out. Based on the current law and on the trend of the government continuing to spend more money than it receives, people can gauge the political climate and the swings of the political pendulum between the left and the right. Given the national debt, it is not unreasonable to come to the conclusion that the federal estate tax is probably going to remain for decades to come.

Now, for the time being, people have a federal estate-tax threshold of $5,250,000, as it was established on January 1, 2013. What that means is that any estate assets worth more than $5,250,000 will be taxed at a 40-percent rate when those assets pass to the next generation. Beyond that, if the estate is being transferred in a state that also imposes an estate tax, that state's estate tax also has to be figured into the equation. For example, New Jersey has a state estate tax on assets of more than $675,000. Suppose you are a resident of New Jersey when you pass away, leaving behind an estate worth $2 million. New Jersey's representatives would say, "Well, we want approximately $99,200 in New Jersey estate taxes." The federal government's representatives, if that $1 million threshold had become a reality, would have said, "Anything more than $1 million is taxed at 55 percent. You left an estate worth $2 million; there is a 55-percent tax on the excess beyond $1 million." That is another $550,000 that you would have effectively left to Uncle Sam.

The good news here is that the federal estate-tax threshold did not go back to $1,000,000. Instead it went up to $5,250,000. For married couples who do proper estate planning, the federal threshold is $10,500,000. State estate taxes are still a threat for many because of their much lower threshold. Retirees and pre-retirees also need to take into account the fact that any money in IRAs is still subject to federal and state income tax when it is withdrawn. In addition, the federal government requires the receipt of its estate tax money within 9 months of a person's passing. Sometimes, that can mean an estate sale of real estate or a business at bargain-basement prices, all to raise money to pay estate taxes. It can also mean forced withdrawals from an IRA to pay estate taxes, which trigger additional income taxes on those IRA withdrawals.

The challenge is to find an effective way to protect those assets from too much taxation. Solutions can be found the area of wealth transfer planning, which takes account of the benefit of having either a revocable living trust or an estate-planned will that, for married couples, creates a trust upon the death of the first spouse for the benefit of the surviving spouse. This type of trust is often referred to as a *bypass,* a *B trust,* or a *marital trust.* It can also be created in a revocable living trust. Upon the death of the first spouse, certain assets go into the trust for the benefit of the surviving spouse. As a result, that trust, in effect, gets its own federal and state estate-tax exemptions. By having the proper legal documents in place, retirees and pre-retirees can effectively double the amount of money that is not subject to federal and state estate taxes.

Beyond that, when an estate-planning attorney drafts an individual's will or trust, it is a good idea for that individual to look at the spending habits and family dynamics of the next generation, since a view of those dynamics should inform the planning. For example, people sometimes say to me, "I really love my son/daughter, but I do not completely trust my daughter-in-law/son-in-law." Many follow up with this type of worry: "I know 50 percent of marriages end in divorce. What happens if I leave a substantial amount of money to my son and then he goes through a divorce?"

It is a legitimate concern. Most states follow something called *equitable distribution,* which is basically a division of all the assets that have been accumulated during the marriage between the two divorcing spouses. People do not want the money they have worked a lifetime to generate to fall into the hands of an in-law. What can be done to avoid that scenario?

Suppose you leave money to your adult son and he puts that money into a joint bank account, shared with his spouse, or uses some of that money to pay a joint credit card bill. By doing so, he is likely to have converted that asset into a marital asset, which would be subject to an equitable distribution upon divorce.

One clever and creative technique to avoid the above situation is to create what is called a *sub-trust* in your will or revocable living trust that would put your assets in trust for the benefit of your children and/or grandchildren only. By doing so, you can protect those assets from falling into the hands of divorcing spouses. You can also use this type of trust to protect that money from creditors' claims.

Sometimes, people are concerned because their offspring have high-risk occupations, such as those in the medical field, and they may be subject to some type of lawsuit down the road. People have the desire to protect an inheritance against creditors' claims. A sub-trust can do that.

This is important to consider, since this type of thing does happen. For example, when Charlie, a widower, passed away, he left his assets to his adult son, Tom. Tom subsequently went through a divorce. In that divorce, half of the inheritance Tom had received from Charlie went to Tom's ex-wife, who was having an affair and went on to marry somebody who was a total stranger to Charlie. Yet half of what Charlie had worked a lifetime for ended up in the hands of someone he did not even know (namely, the new husband of Tom's ex-wife). That outcome could have been avoided through proper planning.

The question I often hear when this topic comes up is, "Doesn't it generally cost more in legal fees to have this type of trust documented, as opposed to a regular will?" The answer is yes, since the attorney does more work to create customized options for a specific trust and create provisions for the dispersal of money. Whenever more work is involved, a higher fee is a likely result. It is a question of what makes more sense: pay a little more to the attorney who drafts the documents to have them done properly, or risk having estate money go to people who do not deserve it.

Another common scenario regards the concern that irresponsible children will squander assets. A client may say, "My son is a wonderful person, but, gee, he just can't handle money properly," or "My daughter just can't handle money properly. She spends money like water. My concern is that if she receives this inheritance, it is going to be gone." This is not a baseless concern. In fact, studies suggest it can be the rule rather than the exception. I read a report claiming that 85 percent of inherited IRA money is spent within fourteen months.

If that is a concern for you, there is a solution. An attorney can create *spendthrift provisions,* which allow a trust to disperse money to the heirs over time. In many cases, this may be a wise thing to do in order to protect family members from their own lack of fiscal judgment. It is better to plan for the worst than to do nothing and let the worst happen; it is a sad thing when planning is not done properly and the outcome is different from what was desired.

In another example, one of my clients, Frank, passed away, leaving his estate to his wife, Jill. Six months later, when Jill passed away, assets went equally to their two children, one of whom, Leo, had gambling and drinking problems. Unfortunately, within a year, Leo's inheritance of $1 million was gone.

When this type of conversation comes up, I have heard people say things like, "Well, my son is not a drunkard," or "My son doesn't have a gambling problem." My answer to that is that an heir does not have to have a gambling problem or a drinking problem. He or she just has to have a spending problem.

Sometimes, someone will have an adult child whose spouse spends excessively; in that case, the concern is about protecting the inheritance from that spouse's spending habits. Once again, a trust can be the answer.

Of course, predatory taxes and spendthrift heirs are not the only challenges to keeping an inheritance safe for loved ones. Earlier in this chapter, I gave an example in which I explained how somebody passing away and leaving an estate worth $2 million behind could be subject to more than half a million dollars in federal and state estate taxes, not counting income taxes on IRAs that are inherited and subsequently withdrawn. The question in that situation is what can be done to deal with that tax bill.

The answer is a pretty simple one, and it involves another type of trust: an *irrevocable trust*. This type of trust appeals to people who say, "We've spent a lifetime building up this taxable estate. We've identified what we need for income generation and protection against catastrophic illness for the balance of our lifetime. Now, what we want to do is to start building a non-taxable estate, an asset that will benefit our children and grandchildren, and an asset that will be free of estate and income taxes."

If people do not do proper planning in this area, the government has a plan of its own, which is to take what many would feel is an unfair percentage of the estate assets and, essentially, use the estate tax to redistribute that money to other people's children who, according to the government, may be more needy.

I can give you an example. Frank and Ann are a husband and wife in their early seventies. They came to my office to discuss the fact that Ann had reached age seventy-and-one-half, so she had to take her first required minimum distribution, which was approximately $18,000. Ann asked me, "What do you think I should be doing with this required minimum distribution?"

In response, I asked, "Do you see yourself being unable to meet your income needs under any circumstances? Do you need this money to pay the bills or to spend on anything? Do you need it for any purpose?"

At this point, Frank jumped in and said, "No, we really do not. We've got more than adequate income coming from a combination of my pension, Social Security, investment income, and required minimum distributions from my IRA. This is really excess income."

Looking at the fact that Ann and Frank's total assets were worth about $2 million, my suggestion was that they consider setting up a trust, gifting approximately $10,000 a year into the trust, and having the trustee of the trust, their adult son or daughter, send an annual payment to a life insurance company for second-to-die life insurance. At their age, the $10,000 per year would create more than $500,000 of life insurance money that could be paid out estate- and income-tax-free upon the death of the surviving spouse (the second to die).

Ann, Frank, and I looked at this scenario and determined that if they lived sixteen years or so, the internal rate of return on their net death benefit would be more than 10 percent. They thought that was astonishing. As a result, they decided that taking $10,000 a year of that required minimum distribution and repositioning it through an annual gift to the trust was a wise thing to do. They did not see any reason to take that money and put it in a stock that could go up or down in value, a bond that was likely to go down in value as interest rates rose, or a CD where it would make next to no interest. Instead, they used an effective technique that allowed them to reposition money and, in effect, do wealth transfer planning for the benefit of their family.

Sometimes it is difficult to think about this concept of using life insurance as an estate-planning tool because so many people are taught repeatedly to have just enough low-cost term insurance in place to cover the bills in the event of premature death. If a mortgage needs to be paid off or if children's education is not yet funded, term insurance can step in to fulfill that purpose. When people get older and no longer have worries about mortgages or college educations, conventional wisdom then asks what in the world they need life insurance for. It is just an unnecessary expense. Get rid of it.

What people are coming to understand is that life insurance can be a tax-favored asset under the tax code; thus, when retirees structure a life policy to provide tax-free money to family members down the road, they create tremendous advantages. These policies can be set up to have a minimum annual premium. In other words, people often want to have the least outlay on an annual basis to create the most death benefit.

Sometimes people to whom I suggest this say, "Well, I don't know if I want to have this annual commitment for the next fifteen years or for the balance of my lifetime. Is there any way to accomplish this if I don't want an annual commitment?" The answer is yes, there is.

I can give you an example of a client named Jenny, who had approximately $500,000 in CDs. It did not make any economic sense for her to keep that much money in CDs, especially since the CDs were earning less than 1 percent. She had more than adequate income coming in to meet her needs. The CDs, which she had inherited from her mother, gave her a certain amount of emotional security.

I asked her, "What do you view as the purpose of these CDs?"

She said, "Well, the money is there in case I need it, although I know realistically that I'm probably not going to need it. Really, I guess, it's just going to be a legacy for my children."

I suggested she consider taking half of the money, or even the whole amount, and putting it into a single-premium or single-deposit life plan. Jenny ended up taking out $250,000, which she put into a single-premium life insurance policy. This created a paid-up policy with a death benefit of around $1.1 million.

Now, if Jenny had left that $250,000 in a low-interest CD at today's interest rates, it would have taken in excess of fifty years for it to reach to $1.1 million. When the device of the trust is used to own the policy, the proceeds pass to the family free of estate and income taxes.

Sometimes people say, "Well, I didn't know you could gift that much. I thought you were limited to gifting $13,000 per year." Actually, an individual can gift more than $13,000 per year, provided that his or her accountant files a gift tax return and takes a credit against the estate- and gift-tax threshold in the future.

Again, the purpose behind this book is not to give specific legal or tax advice and have people run out and act based on what they have read in the book. The idea is to encourage readers to talk to a qualified professional – a qualified financial adviser, accountant, or attorney – because laws can be subject to change, and readers want to make sure that they are doing things correctly so that they do not run into an unforeseen problem.

My clients feel pretty comfortable working with me because they know I stay up-to-date on changes in the law and that I work with other professionals, estate-planning attorneys, and accountants who do the same.

I would like to mention one other thing in closing this chapter: Current law presents a situation in which a person can actually gift $5 million without incurring gift tax. For example, if $5 million goes into a single-premium life insurance policy, that second-to-die type of policy means people in their sixties might create $30 or $40 million of tax-free money for their heirs on the back end. Depending on when you read this book, there may be a large gift- and/or estate-planning opportunity for the very affluent. If you are in that category, I strongly suggest you take advantage of it if it makes sense for you and your family.

CHAPTER EIGHT

Must-Have Estate-Planning Documents

When it comes to conducting smart estate-planning, there are some essential estate-planning documents that should be part of everybody's plan. Keep in mind that the information provided in this chapter, while it refers to essential legal documents you should be considering, is not a substitute for proper legal advice. Later in the chapter, I will cover the questions you should ask an estate-planning attorney when interviewing that attorney.

Most people, when they think of estate planning, think primarily of the last will and testament. Certainly, it is important to have a last will and testament, but there are some points to consider regarding that document.

The number-one point would be, of course, those to whom you are leaving your assets. The last will and testament spells that out. In addition, it is important for you to name the person who is going to serve as the executor of your estate in that document. Often, somebody will name his or her spouse as the executor. It is also important to consider naming back-up executors, in the event that the person you name as primary executor is unable or unwilling to serve in that capacity.

In addition, if you are responsible for minor children, it is important that your will spells out who will serve as the guardian of those children until they become of age. Otherwise, they can be made wards of the court and wind up living in foster care until a suitable guardian can be appointed, and that is the last thing you would want to have happen to your grieving children. If you are a parent, even if you do not have much in the way of assets, you can see why that last will and testament is an important document.

The probate process, by which the probate court retitles your assets to your heirs, can be burdensome and time-consuming, depending to some extent on the state in which you live. In some states, and under some circumstances, there are ways of avoiding the delays of probate administration through specific kinds of estate planning. Often, financial planners will recommend using a revocable living trust. With a revocable living trust, you can take your current assets and title them to the name of the trust; then, the trust document will name successor trustees to take over those assets after you pass away. A revocable living trust is not essential in every state. For example, in New Jersey, the probate process is not as burdensome and extensive as it is in many other states. In Florida and many other states where probate can be costly and lengthy, financial planners often recommend a living trust.

Other important legal documents to have include an *advanced medical directive*, which identifies who is authorized to make decisions about your healthcare in the event you are incapacitated. In that area, it is also important to name back-up agents. A *living will* is also important because it spells out under what circumstances you would or would not want to have your life preserved via machinery. For example, you could specify that you do not want a respirator or feeding tube used, or other things of that nature. In some states, the advanced medical directive and the living will are combined into one document.

Another document that it is generally prudent to have in place is a *financial power of attorney*, or a *general power of attorney*, which gives whomever you designate the power to manage your financial affairs in the event you are incapacitated. Obviously, the person you name in that document should be a trustworthy person. Some states allow for what is known as a *springing power of attorney*, which is a power of attorney that springs into effect upon the diagnosis of one or more doctors that you are incapacitated and unable to make decisions. This document is important because you do not want to have a situation in which, let's say, late in life you come down with Alzheimer's disease or senile dementia, you are unable to manage your own affairs, and there is no document that spells out who is to step in and manage your affairs for you. Your family would be forced to hire an attorney, go to court, and petition the court to set up a guardian for you. That could be a very expensive, time-consuming process, which again could be avoided just by having the proper legal documents.

Let's take an example. I recall a lady with whom I worked who was in her early eighties. I had helped her with her financial planning in terms of properly positioning retirement savings for lower fees and expenses, tax savings, and income generation, and she was thrilled with the help that I had provided. I suggested to her that she meet with an estate-planning attorney and have a will and a power of attorney created. The topic was not that important to her because she had never been married. She said, "Well, whatever I leave, I'm leaving to nieces and nephews. I have a will I did myself on forms that I bought in an office-supply store. I don't see the need to spend the money."

What she overlooked, even though I advised her to meet with an attorney, was what would happen if she became mentally incapacitated. She did not draft a power of attorney. Unfortunately, she developed senile dementia and ended up needing to be cared for in an institutional setting. No one had been appointed to handle her affairs via legal documents. No one had power of attorney. Her nephew ended up having to hire an attorney, at a fairly substantial expense, to help get himself appointed by a court as his aunt's guardian. At that point, he had to report back to the court periodically on how her finances were being used for her benefit. All that could have been avoided with proper documents.

I have a personal example to share, too. My father passed away unexpectedly at the age of seventy-seven due to a sudden stroke. At the time he passed away, my father was the primary caregiver to my mother, who suffered from Alzheimer's disease. Because of her condition, my mother lacked the legal capacity to make decisions for herself or to appoint someone to act on her behalf. Fortunately, years earlier, prior to being diagnosed with Alzheimer's, she had created an advanced directive. She had had an attorney draft an advanced directive for healthcare, a living will, and a general power of attorney. In those documents, she named my father as the primary agent and named me as the secondary agent in the event that my father was unable or unwilling to serve. Since my father passed away before my mother did, I was able to step into his shoes to help my mother out.

While I was caring for my mother, I cannot tell you how many representatives of different entities asked to see those documents, whether it was her doctor wanting to be sure I was the person who was able to make healthcare decisions or representatives of the hospital or the Alzheimer's care center. These papers were necessary in many instances, and I avoided many problems, thanks to my mother's foresight. Based on that firsthand experience, I can tell you that it is important and necessary to have the right documents in place; failing to have the right documents in place can create difficulties down the road.

Another important aspect to having your legal house in order is the possible tax savings that can be generated for your heirs. Your legal documents, depending upon the level of assets you have, could contain trust provisions that give you the ability, in effect, to double your estate-tax exemption amount. Typically, this is done through what is known as a marital trust or a bypass trust. This can be set up in the will, in which it is called a *testamentary trust*, since it goes into effect upon the death of the testator or the person drafting the will; alternatively, it can be set up in a revocable living trust.

In such a case, what happens upon the death of the first spouse is that certain assets go into the trust for the benefit of the surviving spouse. The surviving spouse can be the trustee of that trust. There are certain rules to follow, but the bottom line is that this marital trust gets its own estate-tax exemption, so the beneficiaries are able to save substantially on state taxes as a result of using this particular vehicle. Moreover, this is not something just for the extremely wealthy, since some states have relatively low estate-tax exemption amounts. For example, in New Jersey, when any amount worth more than $675,000 is passed to the next generation, it is subject to estate taxes. However, by having a marital trust or bypass trust in the deceased's will, the amount that would not be subject to state estate taxes would double from $675,000 to $1.35 million.

At the time of writing this chapter, the federal estate-tax exemption amount was scheduled to reach $5.25 million on January 1, 2013. Having a bypass trust would allow a couple's estate-tax exemption, in effect, to be doubled from $5.25 million to $10.5 million, in terms of the amount that would not be subject to federal estate taxes.

If you are using a revocable living trust as part of your estate planning, the other document that you should consider in conjunction with it is a *pour-over will*, which specifies that the assets you inadvertently leave out of the trust can pour over, or spill over, into the trust. Keep in mind that you cannot take your IRA and put that into your revocable living trust; if you do so, your action will be considered an income-taxable distribution of all the money in the IRA.

Once again, it is important to get professional advice in this area rather than trying to be a do-it-yourselfer, even though you can find plenty of resources online that will say, "You should do this on your own," or, "You can get the documents done through an online document-preparation service." That is, in my opinion, a risky way for you to go; if the documents are not executed properly, generally your heirs will not discover the problem until you have passed away. Obviously, it can be too late to fix things at that point.

When it comes to hiring an attorney to draft your will, trust, or other legal documents, there are certain things to know and questions you should ask of the attorney. The first thing you want to consider is whether you are dealing with an attorney who specializes in this area. Knowledge today has gotten very, very specialized. If, for example, you have a cardiac problem and need medical advice, you would want to see a cardiologist rather than your general practitioner. The same standards apply when entrusting someone with preparing your vital estate-planning documents. For example, do you want to deal with an attorney who is in traffic court in the morning, is handling a real-estate closing at noon, is working on somebody's divorce in the afternoon, and is writing estate-planning documents as a sideline to his or her other practice? Or, in contrast, do you want to deal with somebody who focuses primarily on the area of estate planning? I think that the answer is pretty obvious.

When you interview the attorney or attorneys you are considering for your estate planning, there are certain things for which you should look. First, when you call the attorney's office, pay attention to how the phones are answered. For instance, do you always get an answering machine, or does a live person pick up the phone? That level of service can be indicative of what your overall experience with that attorney will be.

In addition, at your initial meeting, you need to get that attorney's opinion of what documents you will need and find out exactly what the costs are going to be. Some attorneys will give a free initial consultation, and some will not. It is important to determine what the cost of the initial consultation will be when you set your appointment. Some attorneys also might charge for an initial consultation but then reduce the cost of the documents by the cost of the initial consultation if you decide to engage them.

The other question worth asking is whether the fee that you are paying includes a regular review of your legal documents. Laws can change, and they probably will change in the future. The state and gift tax rules could be altered in ways that might make your documents outdated. What if you want to make changes to the documents later? Ask the attorney, "What is it going to cost to do make such changes?" I think it is important to have an idea right up front of what the attorney's obligation is to you, not just in terms of drawing up the documents, but in terms of revising them to keep up with changing laws or life circumstances. A will you wrote ten or twenty years ago might not accurately reflect your wishes and needs later.

For example, I remember sitting down with a husband and wife one May, shortly before the Memorial Day weekend. This particular couple, who were in their seventies, had a second home on the New Jersey shore. They really enjoyed using their second home because their children and grandchildren went there and spent a great deal of time in the summer with them. These clients were very good clients of mine. That May, we had a review meeting and talked about how the couple had properly positioned their retirement savings to help them better achieve their objectives and provide for specific levels of income. They told me how happy they were with everything that they had done so far.

Then I asked them if they had followed through on the recommendation I had made a year earlier to sit down with an estate-planning attorney and get their legal documents brought up to date. The husband said to me, "Well, no, I haven't. Remind me why I need to do that."

I said to him, "You told me last year that your will was made twenty-five years ago and that it still had provisions for minor children's trusts, even though your kids are all adults now." More importantly, I reminded him that the will did not contain any estate-tax saving provisions. It did not contain any language that would create a marital or bypass trust for the benefit of the surviving spouse, which is the device that allows for a doubling of the amount of money not subject to federal and state estate taxes.

He said, "Oh, yeah. That's right. Yeah. That's important. I need to get that done. I need to take care of that. Do you know what?

We're heading down to the shore the day after tomorrow. I think what I'll do is wait until after Labor Day, after we get back. I'll take care of this in September."

I pointed out, "This is something that is important. If, God forbid, one of you were to pass away, you can't go back in time and do it after the fact."

He kind of chuckled, and said, "Well, I'm not too worried about that."

Shortly after the Fourth of July, I got a phone call from his wife saying that he had passed away the night before. He had suffered a fatal heart attack. His good intentions of getting his estate-planning documents in order and taking advantage of estate-tax savings provisions in his will never came to fruition. That ultimately cost his family tens of thousands of dollars in unnecessary taxes, which could have been avoided.

If you are using a revocable living trust, be sure to clarify the help you will get from your attorney or his or her office in retitling assets into the name of the trust. For example, if you are taking a piece of real estate and retitling it into the trust, who is actually going to be doing that for you? Is there an additional charge for that service? I would establish that up front, because it does not do much good to have a revocable living trust drafted and then not have assets retitled into the name of the trust.

In addition, I think it is important to talk about your family dynamics with the attorney who is drafting your documents, since there may be specific situations that need to be addressed in those documents. If you have an adult son or daughter who is disabled, you will want to talk to the attorney about what is called a *special-needs trust*. This allows you to set money aside for your disabled child's benefit, without disqualifying that child from receiving whatever government benefits to which he or she would otherwise be entitled. If you have an adult son or daughter you feel is likely to blow through any inheritance money immediately, once again you may want to talk to your attorney about creating a trust that would regulate the flow of money over time to that family member.

Find an attorney with whom you are comfortable, with whom you can communicate, and with whom you are able to establish ground rules from the get-go so that there are no surprises in terms of additional costs and fees. It is also important that you understand what these documents do and do not do for you.

Sometimes, when it comes to getting a will done, people can be almost superstitious. Some people feel that if they make a will, they will soon die. It is silly, but sometimes people also feel that there are more fun or more important things to do: "I'll just back-burner this," they say, "because, after all, I can do it at any point in time." No person knows how long he or she is destined to live. As a result, it is prudent to have these documents drawn up.

When you are drafting your legal documents, please do not forget that the choices you make, or do not make, can have a serious impact on family harmony after you're gone. Certainly, none of us wants to think about our loved ones squabbling after we are gone, but it can happen when people fail to make their wishes clear ahead of time. An illustration I can give on this point concerns a family I knew. The mother had many keepsakes or heirlooms: jewelry that had been passed down from her mother and grandmothers, a Hummel collection, and certain artwork. These collectibles were special to her and, I guess, because they were special to her, they were also special to her three daughters. Her will did not spell out who was to get which particular keepsakes. It simply stated that everything was to be divided equally between the three heirs.

Sadly, after the mother passed away, the daughters argued over who was to get which piece of jewelry, who was to get their mother's wedding ring, who was to get the collectible figurines, and who was to get this painting or that painting. Clearly, their mother would have found this outcome very distressing.

Sometimes if a problem is something that can be anticipated, it can be avoided through a *personal property memorandum*, which, in effect, becomes part of the will. This type of memorandum spells out which particular keepsakes or heirlooms go to which people; it can also be referred to as a *specific bequest*. The idea behind it is to maintain family harmony. It is worth considering. Boilerplate documents do not include this feature. Custom-drafted documents can. It is important to discuss this topic frankly with your attorney, and to work with an attorney who is aware of this problem.

DEALING WITH DOCUMENTS

Often, clients ask me, "How long should I be keeping important papers? What papers are important? What papers should I be saving? How long should I be saving them? Where should I keep them?"

A friend of mine went through a challenging experience last year when, on the day after Thanksgiving, his house caught fire because of a defective fireplace. Fortunately, no one was hurt, and the family got their essentials out of the house before the house was destroyed. However, this example is a reminder that it is important to keep and store important documents safely. I strongly recommend that you put together what I call an emergency kit in a file box that has a handle on it. Better yet, invest in a small, fireproof safe that has a handle on it, so you can grab it fast and go in case of an emergency.

Inside, you can store necessary documents, including the following: birth certificates; death certificates; Social Security cards; passports; emergency contact information, such as the names of physicians, contact information for other family members, and names and numbers for your insurance agents; marriage certificates or divorce decrees; your wills; and copies of driver's licenses or other identification cards. In addition, if you are on any lifesaving prescriptions, you will need copies of those. You will also need a list of your bank accounts and credit card account numbers, along with a full inventory of your household goods, including photos of any items of particular value. Think about it. If you did have a house fire, how would you show what you had in the house if everything burned up? That emergency kit needs to be reviewed at least once a year to be sure that everything in it is current and ready to go. It will save you hours of trouble and expense, and it will take a burden off of your shoulders in the unhappy event that you actually need those papers and that information in an emergency. Do not put it off; think of it as a gift to yourself of peace of mind.

When it comes to what to keep in your home filing cabinet, generally you will want to keep the following: credit card statements, medical records, retirement account statements, investment account statements, bills, paycheck stubs, tax returns, bank statements, information on warranties and rebates, copies of your legal documents, wills, and trusts. Things of that nature are important to keep in a file cabinet where you can easily access them. In other words, these are things that you want to file instead of pile, so that if you need to put your hands on them, you will know where they are.

The following question comes up often: "Well, how long should I keep some of these things? Should I have tax returns for the last thirty years?" A rule of thumb when it comes to tax documents is to keep tax returns and supporting documents, such as receipts, real-estate closing statements, 1099s, and W-2s for seven years. The IRS may audit you within three years of suspecting a "good faith errors," six years if you may have underreported your income by at least 25 percent, and within unlimited time if you did not file a return or filed a fraudulent return. Most people do file their returns, so keeping documents for seven years is generally what most experts recommend.

Keep investment records for as long as you own the securities, based on the simple reason that you will want to be able to prove what your cost basis is when you sell a security. You will need to have a record of what you paid for the stock or the bond that you are selling years later so you can prove capital gains and losses. Your brokerage company may be able to provide you with that information if you are stuck, but it is best to have it in hand, particularly if you change brokers.

As far as bank statements go, I do not think it is important to keep those for as long you keep as tax returns. Keep bank statements for just as long as it is necessary for you to check the accuracy of each statement. Generally, people will keep bank statements for one year. I do not think there is a need to keep them for much longer than that. Bear in mind that your bank generally will have statements available to you online.

As far as retirement plan statements are concerned, you generally want to keep those for a year. In contrast, you should keep Roth IRA statements until you retire so that you are able to demonstrate you already paid taxes on the contributions.

Regarding credit card statements, after you have checked to make sure that your statements are accurate, you should shred your statements. The reason I say this is that credit card statements can be a source of identity theft. Unless you need a statement as your only record of a tax-related transaction (because you misplaced or do not have the original receipt), there is no need to keep them for a longer period of time. Again, if you really need to get them, the bank that issues the credit card generally has the statements available to you online.

As far as records of your income for the previous year are concerned, you should keep those until you receive your W-2 and 1099 forms. You ought to keep bills for a year for tax purposes. If you are not yet retired, keep your W-2 and 1099 forms until you begin claiming Social Security, since they are the best estimate of your earnings over the years from which you can calculate the payments to which you are entitled.

CHAPTER NINE

Avoiding Scams, Scam Artists, and Identity Theft

One of the biggest problems in our data-rich society is easy access to people's personal and financial information, an opportunity that criminals exploit every day. Older people are frequently the targets of identity theft, scams, and cons, as well as the targets of dishonest folks who pose as financial advisers, their main aim is to separate clients from their money. Often, people ask me how to avoid investment scams, how to avoid or help prevent identity theft, and how to find a qualified financial adviser. In this chapter, I will explain how you can begin to safeguard yourself from the bad guys targeting your finances.

Identity theft is the fastest-growing crime in America. Hardly a week passes without a news story of another corporation or website that has had its database hacked and the personal information of its clients and customers stolen by cyber criminals. Every year millions of people – literally, millions – become victims of identity theft. It can take a consumer weeks, or sometimes even months or longer, to undo the damage.

Here are some of the best tips you can follow to reduce or prevent identity theft:

- Reduce the number of credit cards that you carry with you.
- When you use a credit or a debit card at a restaurant or store, be sure to take your receipt. Do not leave a receipt that might have your card number information.
- Do not carry your Social Security number in your purse or wallet.
- Do not carry your passport or birth certificate, except when it is absolutely necessary.
- Be careful when giving out your personal information. It is not advisable to give out your personal information over the phone, by mail, or over the Internet, unless you know or have an ongoing relationship with the company with which you are doing business and you have initiated the contact.

I can tell you that I have received scam e-mails from companies pretending to be American Express, Bank of America, and Wells Fargo Bank. These e-mails look absolutely genuine because the scammers use the banks' logos. In these e-mails, the senders claim they are seeking to "verify personal information." I printed out the scam e-mails and took it right to the banks. I asked the bank representatives, "Is this something that your bank sent out?"

In each case, they said no and asked me if they could have the printout, since they wanted to send it to their fraud-prevention department. Just because you get an e-mail that looks real does not mean that it is real. The key to checking suspicious items is making sure that you are the one who initiates the contact and that you call the customer service number shown on your credit card. If you do that, it should be reasonably safe to talk about your personal information. However, if you get a phone call at your house from somebody who claims to be from your bank or your credit card company, do *not* give the caller any information. It is much safer to say, "Give me your number. I'll call you back." Then call the number shown on your bank statement or on your credit card statement.

In addition, it is important to have a shredder and to use it. You can get an inexpensive shredder at any office-supply store. Shred any financial documents or mail containing personal information before discarding them.

I personally do not like the idea of having mail left in my mailbox outside my house. Years ago I had no problem with it; it was convenient. I could just put the outgoing mail in the mailbox, lift the flag up, and let the mailman pick up the mail. Today, the mail sitting in your mailbox, waiting for pickup, might contain a check or a credit card number. If that falls into the wrong hands, you are quite possibly going to end up the victim of identity theft.

I know a young man, a college student, who had his identity stolen. He traced it back to an incident in which he had left his car door unlocked when a copy of his application for financial aid lay on the passenger seat. A financial aid application includes the applicant's Social Security number and other personal information, such as date of birth and bank account numbers. This information was all the thief needed to steal his identity.

In addition, it is important to protect your computer and your e-mail by having a firewall on your home computer to prevent hackers from getting into your hard drive. Install and update your virus protection software to prevent worms or viruses engineered to reveal private information to others from getting into your computer. Typically, the same companies that provide anti-virus protection can also provide firewall protection, and there are many options available to you.

Another very good idea is to remove your name from the marketing list of the three credit-reporting bureaus. Why? The credit-reporting bureaus sell those marketing lists. Sometimes people wonder, "Why do I get so many credit card offers in the mail? How did this bank know that I'm a credit-worthy person?" The reason is that the bank's representatives bought your name from one of the credit bureaus, which set up profiles based on credit scores and then sell names of people living in certain zip codes where the bank or credit card company is looking to sign up new customers. In order to remove your name and information from those lists, you can call this toll-free number: (888) 567-8688. You can also visit the website titled www.optoutpreescreen.com. You would also do well to get your name and phone number on the national Do Not Call List.

Additionally, you need to be aware of and look for signs that something might be wrong. For example, if your monthly credit card statements should have arrived in the mail but did not, you want to call your credit card company; if someone other than you changed the address on your record, you need to let the company know right away. Another big warning would be if any sort of credit denial letter shows up in the mail for no apparent reason and you know you did not apply for credit; another warning comes from any kind of phone call or letter about purchases that you did not make. Someone I know received a letter suggesting he should buy an extended warranty on the new flat-screen TV he had just purchased – only he had not purchased one. Sure enough, somebody had gotten hold of his credit card number and had purchased a flat-screen TV with it.

Another important safeguard is to request and inspect your credit report periodically. What you want to look for are credit inquiries that you did not initiate. Are there any accounts on the report that you did not open? Your credit report will typically show your recent balance on your credit cards. See if there are any balances that do not seem right or do not reflect the purchases you actually made. Legally, the three major credit-reporting bureaus are required to give you a free credit report each year. You can obtain that report by visiting the website titled, www.annualcreditreport.com. You can also call the following toll-free number: (877) 322-8228. It is also advisable to keep track of what you are spending. When your bank statements, billing statements, and credit card statements come in, look at all the charges to see if they are legitimate.

I got a phone call just last week from the Fraud Prevention Department at Discover Card. They were questioning an $11.68 purchase that my wife had made on iTunes. I said, "Why are you questioning an $11.68 purchase?" They explained that sometimes a thief will make large numbers of purchases for small amounts, figuring that the person whose account they are using will not notice or report it. So it is a good idea to look at statements, and it is not a bad idea to keep your charge receipts, which you may need for tax purposes down the road anyway, particularly if you are running a small business. You should compare those receipts against your statement.

In the event you suspect you might be a victim of identity theft, there are some steps you need to take immediately. First, call the credit-reporting agencies (Equifax, Experian, and Transunion), and have them place a fraud alert on your file. That will help prevent an identity thief from opening additional cards in your name. Equifax's phone number is (888) 766-0008, and the website is www.equifax.

com; Experian's phone number is (888) 397-3742, and the website is www.experian.com; Transunion's phone number is (800) 680-7289, and the website is www.transunion.com.

Second, close all affected accounts. A couple of years ago, my family and I were on vacation in Maui, and we took our rental car out to the beach. My wife put her purse in the trunk for safekeeping. I guess some thieves were in the area and saw her do this; they broke into the car and stole her wallet from her purse. Naturally, we immediately called each of the credit card companies – MasterCard, Visa, American Express, Discover, and the bank that had issued my wife's ATM card. We had new cards issued and had the old accounts closed; then, we filed a police report. A year after this happened, my wife got a phone call from the police in Maui, telling her that someone had found her wallet washed up on a beach. Apparently, what the thieves had done was taken the cash out of her wallet and tossed the rest into the ocean. This wallet had floated around Maui for a year before somebody found it and turned it into the police department.

If you see fraudulent charges on your statement, naturally you will want to call your credit card company to dispute them. If your checking account is involved, have the bank stop payment on your checks and open a new checking account. Of course, you should file a police report, because that will provide you with additional proof that identity theft actually occurred. However, the first line of defense is to take the steps I outlined above to reduce the possibility of being a victim of identity theft.

You can also visit some useful websites. The U.S. Federal Trade Commission has an identity theft clearinghouse. The website is at www.consumer.gov/idtheft, and the commission has a toll-free number, too: (877) 438-4338. If there is something shady going on with your mail, contact the U.S. Postal Service at www.usps.com/postalinspectors. A nonprofit called the Identity Theft Resource Center is also helpful; the relevant website is www.idtheftcenter.org, and the relevant phone number is (858) 693-7935.

Additionally, you can subscribe to services such as Life Lock, which will monitor your credit report on a continuous basis. Some banks now offer similar services.

Now, I want to cover investment scams, which have also been very much in the news as of late, since so many retirees have been cheated out of their life savings. You do not want to let anything like that happen to you, and there are proactive steps you can take to avoid being the victim of a scammer. First, do not rush to make decisions. Good financial professionals – investment professionals who offer investment products or insurance products – will be available next week, next month, and next year. Good professionals respect the fact that making important decisions takes time, and they do not pressure you to make snap decisions. In addition, if an investment proposal sounds strange or too good to be true, that is a big red flag. It is important not to take anything on blind faith. You want to have written materials; you want to study them; and you want to ask questions. Do your homework. Do not fall for appearances just because you are looking at a fancy brochure and someone is speaking in a friendly or an authoritative manner. Scam artists often appeal to emotions, so you need to pause, think carefully, and evaluate your options objectively, rather than making a decision based on fear or greed. It is also advisable not to make important decisions at times when you are vulnerable. For example, it is recommended that you should not make major investment decisions when you have lost a spouse or are recovering from a serious illness, since your judgment might be flawed or you might not do the amount of homework that you otherwise would do.

I think it is important you get into the habit of looking carefully at your investment statements when they come in. Look for excessive or unauthorized trading on them. If you have trouble getting access to your money, keep in mind that reputable financial institutions generally do not stall on withdrawal requests.

Never, ever make out a check directly to a financial adviser. I remember that, years ago, I met with a lady who was opening a fixed annuity, and she was putting a fairly large sum into it (approximately $300,000). She wrote out the check and handed it to me. I said, "Thank you," and she got up to leave the office. Then I happened to look at the check and saw she had made it out to me personally. I immediately stopped her and asked her to tear up the check and make it out instead to the insurance company whose annuity she was going to buy. If an "adviser" tells you to make out your check to him or her, rather than to the company for which he or she works, run.

Do your due diligence. You want to know or verify that the adviser with whom you are working is properly licensed. If you are dealing with an unlicensed person, then you are taking a huge risk. Insurance agents have to be licensed with their state's insurance department. Brokers are licensed through the Financial Industry Regulatory Authority (FINRA).

One really good source for checking on a financial adviser with whom you are considering doing business is the National Ethics Association, which has a website at www.ethics.net; you can also call the company's toll-free phone number, which is (800) 282-1831. When representatives of the National Ethics Association do a background check on an individual, they do a criminal background check, a civil background check, and a credentials check. They also do a professional license check, along with a check to see whether there have been complaints against that individual – is the individual adhering to a professional code of ethics? They will do a Securities and Exchange Commission check, a state department of insurance check, a FINRA check, and a state security administrators check. If you are dealing with an accountant or a real estate professional, they will check with those agencies as well. The National Ethics Association functions like a clearinghouse in that you can call one number to verify all these background checks, since anybody who has worked with them as an adviser has gone through a seven-year background check.

What are some of the most common financial scams seen today? Surprisingly, many otherwise savvy, well-educated people fall for some very old-fashioned scams. Take a Ponzi scheme, for instance, which still shows up periodically. A Ponzi scheme is really an investment pyramid that promises incredible returns. What happens in a Ponzi scheme is that later investors' money is used to pay early investors. Then the promoter goes back to early investors looking for referrals, since the early investors typically are happy with the returns promised. However, the Ponzi scheme's inevitable collapse leaves everyone connected with it poorer, except the promoter. The promoters of Ponzi schemes usually get caught, but by then they have probably spent most or all of the investors' money.

Another thing to look out for is promissory notes. These often look like official certificates guaranteeing above-market, fixed interest rates and protected principal. Frequently, however, these promissory notes are worthless, and the borrower or the person issuing the note may have no intention of repaying the money or may not have the ability to repay it. Affinity fraud is yet another common scam whereby con artists may use their victims' ethnic background or religious background to gain trust. Just because somebody says, "I'm affiliated with your church group" does not mean that you should not do your homework on that person, just as you would on any others who wanted to get their hands on your money.

Another thing to watch out for is unregistered securities. Legitimate investment products must be registered with securities agencies, and unregistered products are something to which you should pay close attention. I have heard many people say, "How did Bernie Madoff get away with what he did for so long?" Well, keep in mind that one thing Bernie Madoff's firm was doing was serving as the custodian for investors' accounts, so the firm was able to print up fraudulent statements on a monthly basis. That should have been a red flag to those investors, but when people think they are making big, easy money, they are not always as critical in their scrutiny of these things as they ought to be.

Always deal with financial advisers who use a reputable third-party institution (such as Fidelity Investments, Charles Schwab, or insurance firms, for example) as the custodian of investments. You do not want to see investments held directly at the financial adviser's firm.

Often, scammers will play on your emotions in order to get you to part with your money, creating a fake emergency that requires you to make a quick decision under emotional duress. One such scam targets elderly people. Here is how it works: your phone rings, and you pick up the receiver to hear a young girl or young boy weeping. The child calls you "Grandma" (or "Grandpa") and says he or she went on a spring break trip with his or her friends, got arrested, and needs bail right now, but is afraid to call his or her parents. He or she asks you to send money immediately via Western Union. Amazingly, this scam works. These scammers probably have to make quite a few phone calls, but they score often enough with upset grandparents to make it worth their while.

Internet scams include e-mails from somebody in a foreign country, such as Nigeria, notifying you that a long-lost relative has left you an inheritance, and you need to post a bond to have the funds transferred from the foreign country into your bank account. The senders of these e-mails want your bank account information, and they want you to wire $5,000 or $10,000 to an overseas account so you can get your million-dollar inheritance. Many people fall for that type of scam, too.

I actually had a client call me to say that he had gotten a phone call from an attorney claiming he was calling from Scotland to tell my client he had inherited a substantial sum of money from a long-lost great-uncle, and my client was the only living relative. The caller wanted my client's bank account information and asked him to wire money. I told my client that this was a scam, and he reported it to the FBI. Some scammers hack into other people's e-mail addresses and use them to write to family members and ask for money, typically to cover a vacation emergency or some sudden medical bills. Please, if you receive such an e-mail, call the person whose name is on the e-mail and make sure that the request is genuine before you send anyone your bank information or credit card number.

The bottom line is, if it sounds too good to be true, or if you are being pressured to make a quick decision or asked to provide personal or financial information by someone you do not know, you are quite possibly being scammed, whether it is via an e-mail or an investment "opportunity" offered by an unscrupulous adviser. A good financial adviser adheres to an ethical code of conduct and works with reputable companies. A good financial adviser encourages you to check his or her background or use the National Ethics

Association to check him or her out. Anyone who deviates from that ethical code of conduct is someone of whom you should be wary.

CHAPTER TEN

Are You Being Served?

I n our society today, it seems as if people are constantly being encouraged to do things themselves. However, you would not try to fill your own teeth, or take out your own appendix, and you really should not be your own financial adviser.

Now, you may say, "Well, I know what I'm doing. I've accumulated substantial assets." That is certainly a legitimate observation. However, is your spouse as knowledgeable as you are in this area? If you pass away first, your spouse may not be able to manage a portfolio the way that you could, and that can put the surviving spouse's financial security at serious risk. In addition, even if you are a self-taught expert, it is good to have a qualified financial adviser to act as a sounding board and to bounce ideas around with you. Remember, it is a financial adviser's business to stay current on all the ramifications of wealth management and estate planning. A good financial adviser can suggest strategies or instruments of which you might not have been aware. My most important suggestion for you here is to urge you to find a qualified adviser with whom you can work. The idea is not to give up control; I am not saying that you should not continue to make your own decisions, but rather that you should obtain informed guidance and input as to what choices are available to you.

As I explained earlier, people do not know what they do not know. Many times, after I have met with people, even the most knowledgeable of them will admit, "I didn't know that there were these particular ways to accomplish my goals, protect my assets, minimize my taxes, or enhance my retirement security through income planning. I didn't know about these techniques." Clearly, if people are unaware that something exists, they cannot take advantage of it. If there were a coupon in the newspaper for $5 off at the supermarket and you did not know it was there, you would not be able to take advantage of it. The same thing is true when it comes to financial advisers. People often do not know that there are advisers who focus exclusively on the needs of retirees or pre-retirees.

Sometimes people think all financial advisers are alike, and that they all are in the business of trying to sell something. If they had a bad experience with a financial adviser who made inappropriate recommendations, they think that all financial advisers are going to make inappropriate recommendations. That is the wrong conclusion to draw. If you had an automobile that was a lemon, would it be right to draw the conclusion that all cars are lemons and never drive a car again?

What you want to do is look for an adviser who has the right qualifications to guide you:

- The adviser should have knowledge of the tax code.
- The adviser should have a broad knowledge of retirement income-planning techniques.
- The adviser should not rely exclusively on the traditional portfolio theory, which is that if just the right amount of assets are diversified, everything should be okay.
- The adviser should be able to think outside the box.

Today people are generally looking for more by way of guarantees, particularly when it comes to meeting income needs. When you are looking for the right advice-giver, it is important to find and hire the best adviser for your particular, unique goals.

The first step is to acknowledge that the rules of the retirement-planning game are changing rapidly. Things are quite different now than they were in your parents' generation or your grandparents' generation. Do not try to go it alone; instead, find an adviser who can do a complete review for you, one who also works with a team of specialized professionals. For example, in our office we have access to a team of certified financial planners who help us do analyses for clients.

The second step is to be aware that if something sounds too good to be true, it probably is. Unfortunately, there are no do-overs when it comes to retirement. If you make bad choices or lose your retirement savings as a result of bad advice, it is not as if you can go back to work for another thirty years and earn the money all over again. When you hear something that sounds good and you want to believe it, ask this simple question: What strings are attached? If somebody tells you there are no strings attached, you should really get up and run out of that person's office.

The third step is to be cautious about taking legal advice from non-lawyers. Get advice from professionals who are licensed in the areas in which they give advice. Just as you do not want to take accounting advice from somebody who is not licensed as an accountant, you do not want to take legal advice from somebody who is not licensed as an attorney.

By the same token, you do not want to take financial advice from someone who is not licensed as a financial adviser. I think it is important to find an adviser who works with a team of professionals in which there is collaboration among like-minded specialists. If you have a good financial adviser who works closely with a skilled state-planning attorney who, in turn, works closely with an accountant, you are lucky; that team approach is extremely valuable, since no single professional can wear all of those hats and be good at all of those jobs.

The Internet has opened up a world of information to most of us. Not all information is created equal, however. It is very important to be careful when it comes to online resources and their trustworthiness. There is a problem today in our society: information overload. For example, if you enter the key words *retirement advice* on Google, you will come up with more than 64 million articles, websites, and resources to consider. While you do need to do research and the Internet can be useful in that effort, any research that you do should be discussed with your qualified financial adviser to see if the information you found online really applies to your particular situation and is factual, or if it differs from the advice your professional gives you.

When you are looking for a financial adviser, I think you have a right to demand proof that the financial adviser with whom you are working is properly licensed and credentialed. Do not just take his or her word for it; trust, but verify. As I mentioned in a previous section, the National Ethics Association is a third-party organization that monitors and does background checks on financial advisers, particularly financial advisers who work with older people. You can visit their website at www.ethics.net. No matter whom you are thinking of working with, check that adviser out first through this association. The association's toll-free number is (800) 282-1831.

I would also look to see that the financial adviser has some demonstrated knowledge in the area in which he or she works. For example, has he or she published on the subjects with which he or she deals? Writing a book is not an easy thing, and someone who takes the time to write clearly about his or her area of expertise generally has a passion for what he or she is doing. Furthermore, you can check his or her book against his or her in-person advice to see if that advice is in line with the message in the book. In addition, I would ask the financial adviser with whom you are considering working whether he or she invests in professional knowledge. Does he or she stay up-to-date through continuing education?

Ask these questions, too: Does your potential adviser get much of his or her business via referrals from other business professionals? Is he or she the go-to person to whom accountants and attorneys refer their clients for retirement income planning?

Lastly, I think it makes sense to trust your feelings and your intuition. I think a great deal is revealed when you can sit down with someone and meet face-to-face to talk about what is important to you and how you feel about what you are trying to accomplish.

My philosophy is to always treat a client as if he or she were a member of my family. My father gave me very good advice years ago, when I first got started working with older people as a financial adviser. Keep in mind that I was in my twenties when I started doing this. What Dad said to me was, "Ron, any time that you sit down with prospective clients, I want you to stop for a minute and just pretend that it is your mother and me sitting across the table from you. If you do that, you will never go wrong." I took that advice to heart and practice it on a daily basis, and it has served me very well.

The complete planning-review process that my colleagues and I go through with every client is extremely valuable. However, I do not think there is a way to express in words or in a book how deeply we care about our clients. That is something that can only come through interaction over time, and I think trust is something that is earned over time as well. It is important that you find a good adviser you can trust, someone who will put your needs first and who will treat you like family.

Unfortunately, my colleagues and I cannot work with everybody who would like to work with us. There are only so many hours in the day. However, I hope that this book and the information it contains is helpful to you in finding the right adviser with whom to work. My firm's website, www.ronaldgelok.com, has more information you can use, too, and I hope you will visit it. The office toll-free number is (800) 467-8152. If you would like to discuss your concerns with our team, we would love to hear from you.

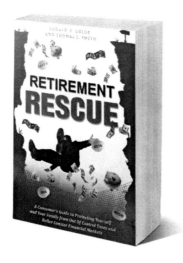

How can you use this book?

MOTIVATE

EDUCATE

THANK

INSPIRE

PROMOTE

CONNECT

Why have a custom version of *Retirement Rescue*

Build personal bonds with customers, prospects, employees, donors, and key constituencies

- Develop a long-lasting reminder of your event, milestone, or celebration
- Provide a keepsake that inspires change in behavior and change in lives
- Deliver the ultimate "thank you" gift that remains on coffee tables and bookshelves
- Generate the "wow" factor

Books are thoughtful gifts that provide a genuine sentiment that other promotional items cannot express. They promote employee discussions and interaction, reinforce an event's meaning or location, and they make a lasting impression. Use your book to say "Thank You" and show people that you care.

Retirement Rescue is available in bulk quantities and in customized versions at special discounts for corporate, institutional, and educational purposes. To learn more please contact our Special Sales team at:

1.866.775.1696 • sales@advantageww.com • www.AdvantageSpecialSales.com